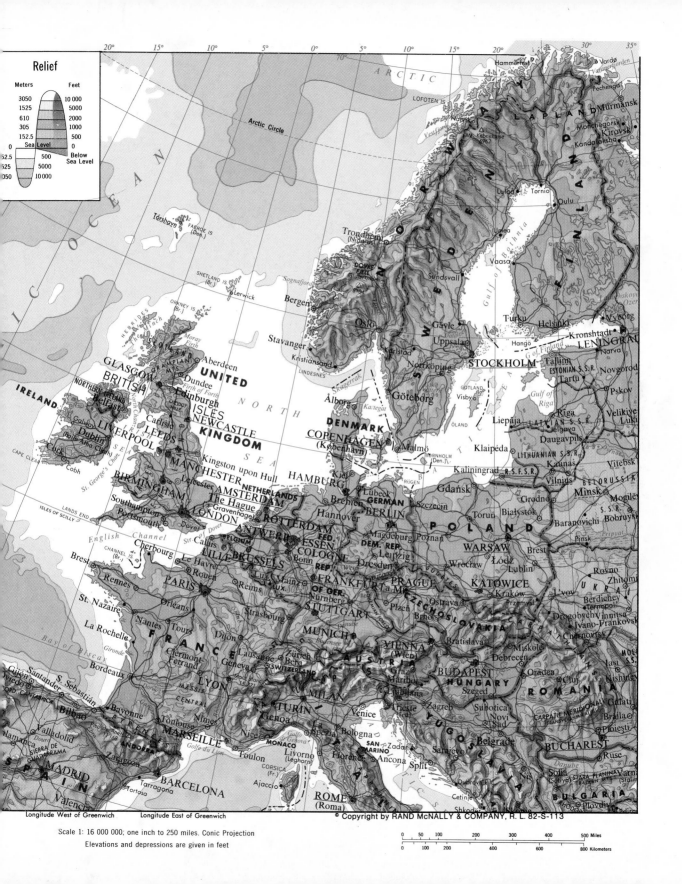

Relief

Meters	Feet
3050	10 000
1525	5000
610	2000
305	1000
152.5	500
0 Sea Level	0
	Below Sea Level
52.5	500
525	5000
050	10 000

Arctic Circle

A R C T I C

ARCTIC OCEAN

LOFOTEN IS

Hammerfest
Vardø
Vadsøfjorden
Pechenga
Murmansk
Monchegorsk
Kirovsk
Kandalaksha

Narvik
LAPLAND

N O R W A Y
S W E D E N
F I N L A N D

Trondheim
(Nidaros)

Vestfjord

DOVRE FJELL
Galdhöpiggen
8104

Sognafjord

Luleå
Tornio
Oulu

SHETLAND IS (Br.)
Lerwick

Bergen
Sundsvall
Vaasa

ORKNEY IS (Br.)

HEBRIDES
Moray Firth
Oslo
Gävle
Turku
Helsinki
Vyborg
Kronstadt
LENINGRAD

Stavanger
Uppsala
Hangö
Narva

Aberdeen
Kristiansand
Norrköping
Tallinn
ESTONIAN S.S.R.
Novgorod

GLASGOW
BRITISH
SCOTLAND
GRAMPIAN MTS
Dundee
UNITED
Firth of Forth
Edinburgh
ISLES
NEWCASTLE
KINGDOM

IRELAND
NORTHERN IRELAND
Belfast
Carlisle
N O R T H
STOCKHOLM
Karlstad
Göteborg
GOTLAND
Visby
ÖLAND
Ps0v

Galway
Dublin
LIVERPOOL
LEEDS
S E A
Ålborg
Kattegat
Liepāja
Riga
Velikiye Luki

Cork
Cobh
BIRMINGHAM
MANCHESTER
Kingston upon Hull
DENMARK
COPENHAGEN
(København)
Malmö
Klaipėda
LATVIAN S.S.R.
Jelgava
Daugavpils
Vitebsk

CAPE CLEAR
St. George's Chan.
Leicester
AMSTERDAM
NETHERLANDS
HAMBURG
Kiel
BORNHOLM (Den.)
Kaliningrad
R.S.F.S.R.
LITHUANIAN S.S.R.
Kaunas
Vilnius
BELORUSSIA
Minsk
Mogilev

ISLES OF SCILLY
LANDS END
Southampton
Portsmouth
The Hague
Gravenhage
LONDON
Dover
Str. of Dover
Calais
ANTWERP
BELGIUM
ROTTERDAM
Bremen
Hannover
BERLIN
Lübeck
GERMAN
DEM. REP.
Szczecin
Gdańsk
Toruń
Białystok
Grodno
S.S.R.
Baranovichi
Bobruysk

English Channel
CHANNEL IS (Br.)
Cherbourg
Le Havre
LILLE
BRUSSELS
COLOGNE
ESSEN
Bonn
FED. REP. OF GER.
Magdeburg
Poznań
Leipzig
Dresden
POLAND
WARSAW
Brest
Pinsk
Pripyat

Brest
Rennes
Rouen
Reims
LUX.
Mainz
FRANKFURT a.M.
Nürnberg
Leipzig
Wrocław
Łódź
Lublin
Rovno
Zhitomir

St. Nazaire
PARIS
Orléans
Strasbourg
STUTTGART
PRAGUE
CZECHOSLOVAKIA
Plzeň
Brno
Ostrava
KATOWICE
Kraków
Przemyśl
L'vov
Berdichev
Ternopol
UKRA

Nantes
Tours
Dijon
Lausanne
Zürich
Bern
MUNICH
Bodensee
Danube
Bratislava
Miskolc
Drogobych
Vinnitsa
Ivano-Frankovsk
Chernovtsy

La Rochelle
F R A N C E
Clermont-Ferrand
Geneva
SWITZERLAND
Mont Blanc
15781
VIENNA
(Wien)
A U S T R I A
Graz
Debrecen
Oradea
Cluj
MOL
S.S.

Bordeaux
LYON
MASSIF CENTRAL
MILAN
TURIN
Venice
Trieste
Maribor
Ljubljana
Zagreb
BUDAPEST
H U N G A R Y
Szeged
Subotica
Novi Sad
ROMANIA
Iaşi
Kishinev

Gijón
S. Sebastián
Santander
Bayonne
PYRENEES
ANDORRA
Nîmes
MONACO
Genoa
La Spezia
Bologna
SAN MARINO
Ancona
Zadar
Split
Sarajevo
Y U G O S L A V I A
Belgrade
BUCHAREST
Ruse

Oviedo
Bilbao
Valladolid
Douro
SIERRA DE GUADARRAMA
Zaragoza
Toulouse
MARSEILLE
Foulon
CORSICA (Fr.)
Livorno
(Leghorn)
Florence
Golfo di Genova
Golfe du Lion

Salamanca
MADRID
S P A I N
Tarragona
Tortosa
BARCELONA
Ajaccio
ROME
(Roma)
Niş
STARA PLANINA (Stalin)
Varna

Valencia
Danube
Sofia
(Sofiya)
B U L G A R I A
Plovdiv

Cetinje
Dubrovnik
Shkodër
Skopje

Longitude West of Greenwich   Longitude East of Greenwich   © Copyright by RAND McNALLY & COMPANY, R. L. 82-S-113

Scale 1: 16 000 000; one inch to 250 miles. Conic Projection
Elevations and depressions are given in feet

| 0 | 50 | 100 | 200 | 300 | 400 | 500 Miles |

| 0 | 100 | 200 | 400 | 600 | 800 Kilometers |

SHETLAND ISLANDS

UNST
Burravoe
Ronas Hill
450
YELL
FETLAR
YELL
St. Magnus Bay
WHALSAY
MAINLAND
Melby House
FOULA
Lerwick
BRESSAY
SHETLAND ISLANDS
Virkie
SUMBURGH HEAD

FAIR ISLE

PAPA WESTRAY
WESTRAY
NORTH RONALDSAY
ROUSAY
North Sound
Westray Firth
SANDAY
EDAY
STRONSAY
ORKNEY ISLANDS
MAINLAND
SHAPINSAY
Stromness
Kirkwall
Ward Hill
481
HOY
Scapa Flow
BURRAY
SOUTH RONALDSAY
Burwick

C

RONA

OUTER HEBRIDES
BUTT OF LEWIS
Barvas
Carloway
ISLE OF LEWIS
Stornoway
Balallan
SCARP
HARRIS
Olisham
799
Tarbert
TARANSAY
SHIANT ISLANDS
PABBAY
BERNERAY
NORTH UIST
HEISKER ISLANDS
BENBECULA
RONAY
SOUTH UIST
Lochboisdale
ERISKAY
VATERSAY
BARRA
MINGULAY
SANDRAY

CAPE WRATH
Durness
STRATHY POINT
DUNNET HEAD
STROMA
CASTLE OF MEY
DUNCANSBY HEAD
John o' Groats
Melvich
Reay
Castletown
Thurso
Halkirk
Tongue
Sinclair's Bay
Ben Hope
927
Scourie
EYE PENINSULA
Wick
Eddrachillis Bay
Leirg
Lybster
Lochinver
Morven
705
Enard Bay
Helmsdale
Ben More Assynt
998
Brora
Ullapool
Golspie
Bonarbridge
Domoch
Dornoch Firth
Portmahomack
Beinn Dearg
1081
Tain
HIGHLAND
Invergordon
Lossiemouth
Buckie
Portsoy
Rosehearty
KINNAIRD'S HEAD
Uig
Cromarty
Burghead
Banff
Macduff
Fraserburgh
Dingwall
Fortrose
Nairn
Forres
Elgin
Aberchirder
Torridon
Beauly
Rothes
Keith
Turriff
Peterhead
1151
Loch Maree
Inverness
Huntly
BUCHAN NESS
Portree
Stromeferry
Insch
Oldmeldrum
ISLAND OF SKYE
Kyle of Lochalsh
Grantown-on-Spey
Ellon
RAASAY
GRAMPIAN
Inverurie
993
Ben Attow
1032
Aviemore
Peterculter
Broadford
Aberdeen
MONADHLIATH MOUNTAINS
Ben Macdui
1309
SOAY
CANNA
Fort Augustus
CAIRNGORM MTS.
Ballater
Banchory
Balmoral Castle
RHUM
Mallaig
Glas Maol
1068
Stonehaven
EIGG
Inverbervie
MUCK
Fort William
1343
Brechin
Laurencekirk
POINT OF ARDNAMURCHAN
Ben Nevis
Pitlochry
COLL
Ballachulish
Kirriemuir
Montrose
TIREE
Tobermory
Forfar
Lochaline
GRAMPIAN MOUNTAINS
Aberfeldy
Blairgowrie
Arbroath
SKERRYVORE
Ben Lawers
3214
Coupar Angus
Carnoustie
29
ISLAND
Craignure
Ben More
967
Dundee
Broughty Ferry
INCHCAPE
IONA
OF MULL
ULVA
Crieff
Newport
ERRERA
Oban
Ben More
1174
St. Andrews
DUBH ARTACH
LUING
Callander
Comrie
Cupar
FIFE NESS
Inveraray
Auchterarder
Perth
COLONSAY
SCARBA
Dunblane
Kinross
Aberdour
Buckhaven
ORONSAY
Ardlussa
Stirling
Alloa
Kirkcaldy
44
Lochgilphead
Alloa
Dunfermline
Cowdenbeath
North Berwick
Helensburgh
Dunoon
CENTRAL
Falkirk
Haddington
Port Askaig
Dumbarton
Greenock
GLASGOW
Edinburgh
ST. ABB'S HEAD
JURA
Tarbert
Paisley
Bathgate
Eyemouth
ISLAY
Rothesay
Coatbridge
Berwick-upon-Tweed
GIGHA ISLAND
Largs
Motherwell
Duns
HOLY ISLAND
Claonaig
Millport
East Kilbride
Hamilton
Lauder
FARNE ISLANDS
Port Ellen
Saltcoats
Lanark
Galashiels
Coldstream
Kilmarnock
Peebles
Kelso
North Sunderland
Irvine
Biggar
Selkirk
Newtown St. Boswells
Galston
Broad Law
840
Melrose
Jedburgh
The Cheviot
815
ISLAND OF ARRAN
Troon
Prestwick
Hawick
Alnwick
MALIN HEAD
INISHTRAHULL
Ayr
Cumnock
Sanquhar
Moffat
NORTHUMBERLAND NATIONAL PARK
Rothbury
Amble
Campbeltown
Maybole
Langholm
Bellingham
Morpeth
Wansbeck
Cardonagh
KINTYRE
MULL OF KINTYRE
Girvan
Thornhill
Lockerbie
Blyth
Moville
AILSA CRAIG
Merrick
843
New Galloway
Whitley Bay
Buncrana
SANDA ISLAND
Lochmaben
Newcastle upon Tyne
Portrush
FAIR HEAD
Tynemouth
Portstewart
RATHLIN ISLAND
Dumfries
South Shields
Ballycastle
Carrickfergus
52
Coleraine
Limavady
Ballymoney
New Galloway
Castle Douglas
Annan
Haltwhistle
Gateshead
Sunderland
Londonderry
MILLEUR POINT
Newton Stewart
Dalbeattie
Gretna
Carlisle
Consett
GAL
Strabane
680
Sawel Min.
Ballymena
Larne
Stranraer
Wigtown
Kirkcudbright
ABBEY HEAD
Solway Firth
Durham
Seaham
Peterlee
Antrim
Carrickfergus
Luce Bay

NORTH SEA

Enchantment of the World

SCOTLAND

By Dorothy B. Sutherland

Consultant: Hereward Senior, Ph.D., Professor of History, McGill University, Montreal, Canada

Consultant for Reading: Robert L. Hillerich, Ph.D., Bowling Green State University, Bowling Green, Ohio

16,656

CHILDRENS PRESS ®

CHICAGO

Changing of the guard at Edinburgh Castle

Library of Congress Cataloging in Publication Data

Sutherland, Dorothy B.
    Scotland.

    (Enchantment of the world)
    Includes index.
    Summary: Describes the geography, history, interesting
sites, daily life, and other aspects of Scotland.
    1. Scotland—Juvenile literature. [1. Scotland]
I. Title. II. Series.
DA762.S77 1985   941.1   85-23227
ISBN 0-516-02787-5   AACR2

Picture Acknowledgments
Hillstrom Stock Photos
©**1984 by Cameramann Int'l., Ltd:** Pages 4, 58, 59 (right),
62 (top), 68, 77 (left), 89, 94
©**1984 Southern Stock Photos:** Page 6 (bottom)
©**Mary Ann Brockman:** Pages 82, 104
©**E. J. Flickinger:** Pages 9 (right), 35 (left)
Roloc Color Slides: Pages 5, 6 (top), 12 (right), 14 (top), 17
(2 photos), 19 (left), 23 (right), 26 (bottom), 30, 46, 50, 61
(top & middle), 63, 72, 79 (left), 83 (2 photos), 84 (right
center), 87 (right), 88
Martin Hintz, Photographer: Pages 9 (left), 21, 22,
29, 51 (left), 74 (right), 77 (right), 78 (2 photos), 84 (left &
bottom), 86, 90, 93, 96, 97

Jerome Wyckoff: Page 10
D.A. Rothermel: Pages 11, 74 (left), 84 (top)
Gladys J. Peterson: Page 12 (left)
Tom Stack & Associates/Spencer Swanger: Pages 14
(bottom), 18, 23 (left)
Paula Zwintscher: Page 19 (right)
Root Resources
©**Roger J. Naser:** Page 20
©**Grace H. Lanctot:** Page 62 (bottom)
©**K. Rapalee:** Page 107
Nawrocki Stock Photo
©**D. Variakojis:** Pages 25, 26 (top), 61 (bottom)
©**1984 Dave Brown:** Cover, pages 42 (right), 44, 70, 79
(right), 87 (left), 95
British Tourist Authority: Pages 28, 99
Historical Pictures Services, Inc. Chicago: Pages 32, 33, 34
(2 photos), 35 (right), 38, 43 (2 photos), 47 (2 photos), 51
(right), 53 (left), 100 (2 photos), 101, 102 (2 photos)
Virginia Grimes: Pages 36, 123
The Granger Collection: Pages 41, 42 (left), 53 (right), 55
Chip/Rosa Maria Peterson
Phyllis A. Messenger: Page 56
©**3rd Coast Stock Source**
©**Alan Magayne-Roshak:** Pages 59 (left), 61 (top left), 73
Colour Library International: Pages 64, 65, 66, 69, 71
Len Meents: Maps pages 15, 18, 22, 54
Courtesy Flag Research Center, Winchester,
Massachusetts 01890: Flag on back cover
Cover: Cawdor Castle

The village of Luss on Loch Lomond

TABLE OF CONTENTS

Rugged mountains are found in the north of Scotland. The Applecross Hills (above) have one of the steepest roads in Britain with hairpin turns to keep a driver alert. In the Highlands is the gloomy Pass of Glen Coe, where a massacre took place in 1692.

Chapter 1

WHA'S LIKE US?

The first thing to know about Scotland is that it is not part of England, although it is joined to it. It is part of Great Britain, or the United Kingdom, or the British Isles. The people are called Scots or Scottish. They will accept being called Scotch and will admit to being British, but don't ever call them English.

The Scots and the English spent more centuries fighting one another than they have living in peace—it is less than two hundred fifty years since the last battle was fought at Culloden in the north of Scotland. While nowadays the similarities between the two countries far outweigh the differences, these differences are rooted in history and tradition. The Scots are very nationalistic and like to think that the harshness of their history and the ruggedness of their land have built a toughness of character that sets them apart. When they celebrate together, they frequently offer this toast: "Here's tae us—wha's like us?"

THE GUID SCOTS TONGUE

If you should go to Scotland, you would have no trouble remembering that it is not part of England, for you would hear people talking with a very different accent. It is easy to get used to the accent, but some people may seem to be talking a different language. In fact, words are often used that don't exist in English. (Words like *guid,* which is pronounced "gid" and means "good.") In remote northern parts of the country or on some of the Western Isles, you will hear people talking Gaelic, which *is* a completely different language—and a language that even few Scots understand.

You probably already know at least one phrase of the dialect, or "guid Scots tongue," as chances are you have heard "Auld Lang Syne" sung on New Year's Eve. That phrase means "old long since," or "long ago." The words to the song were written by Robert Burns, Scotland's most famous poet.

A phrase you probably don't know, but one that will come in very handy if you take a trip to Scotland, is *a wee smirr of rain.* It means "a gentle fall of rain," and visitors must be prepared for a lot of that. There is a saying in Scotland: "If you can see across the *loch* [lake], it's a sign that it's going to rain; and if you can't see across the loch, it's already raining." However, the Scots do not let the rain depress them and one of them, Charles Macintosh, was inspired by it to invent the raincoat. (Strangely, the English call a raincoat a mackintosh, or mac. The Scots call it a waterproof.)

LAND OF THE (ALMOST) MIDNIGHT SUN

The rain helps make Scotland a very beautiful place. Plants and flowers thrive on the moisture. Fuchsias (believed, in the old days, to ward off witches) grow on bushes in country gardens. In the spring rhododendrons, in marvelous shades of pink, red, and violet, grow everywhere. In the fall purple heather carpets the mountains. Parks, public squares, and country railway stations are

Rhododendrons (left) and heather (right) thrive in the moist climate.

ablaze with color and, as the Scots are great gardeners, even quite small houses have lovingly tended flower beds out front.

Of course, the sun shines in Scotland, too. And in summer it shines for a long time. Because of the country's northerly position, daylight in June lasts for as many as eighteen to twenty hours, depending upon how far north one goes. On the Shetlands, the islands off the extreme north of the land, it is never completely dark all night long at midsummer. Throughout the country in summer, even after the sun has set, there are hours of twilight or, as the Scots call it, "the gloaming." A famous Scots entertainer, Sir Harry Lauder, made his fortune singing about "Roamin' in the Gloamin'."

Stirling Castle was built during the sixteenth century.

CASTLES AND CLANS

If you should be in Scotland in summer, then you will have plenty of daylight time in which to explore—and many places are worth exploring. If you would like to see castles, for instance, you won't ever have far to look for them. The Scots, once upon a time, were a very warlike people. When they weren't fighting the English, they were fighting one another. Not only did various kings build castles and palaces, but many noble families also had strongholds from which they could defend themselves against their many enemies.

Sometimes castles are a dominant part of a city, as in Edinburgh or Stirling. Many are in excellent repair and some even lived in. But perhaps the most romantic ones of all are the remote and ruined ones that are monuments to what the English poet William Wordsworth, writing about the Highlands, called "old, unhappy, far-off things, and battles long ago."

Dunvegan Castle is the home of the Clan MacLeod.

Many of the battles long ago were fought by the clans in the Highlands of Scotland. The word *clan* comes from the Gaelic *clann* meaning "children." The Highland clans were really extended families. The head of the clan was called the chief and the clan members were both his tenants and his relatives. The chief had complete rule over the clan, but the system was not the same as the feudal system in England and Europe in which the lord of the manor commanded serfs whom he thought of as inferiors. The Highland clan chief was considered to be the father of his clan, and its members, although they would loyally support him, did not bow down to him. They were thought of as his sons, which is why so many Scottish names begin with *Mac*, which means "son of."

It is not unusual to see males wearing traditional tartan kilts in Scotland.

Each of the tartans for which Scotland is famous is nowadays related to a specific clan. It is likely, however, that in the old days the various patterns derived from different districts and that members of the same clan did not necessarily all wear the same tartan. There are now more than 250 patterns of tartan—classified as ancient, dress, and hunting—many of which are of comparatively recent, nineteenth-century design.

Which brings us to the kilt. Originally the kilt was just a length of cloth, 5 by 15 feet (1.5 x 4.6 meters), that the Highlander pleated and wrapped around his body, with one end pulled over his shoulder and the whole belted at the waist. It could also be used as a sleeping bag. The modern kilt is beautifully made, pleated at the back so that the pattern is preserved, resulting in a very thick, warm garment that never really wears out. A man has a kilt for life. Hanging from the waist, down the front of the kilt, is a *sporran*, which is really a receptacle for the kinds of things that would be kept in the pockets of an ordinary suit. The sporran can be anything from a simple leather pouch to an ornate furred, tasseled, silver-ornamented affair.

The kilt is still seen on Scottish streets, among the business suits and blue jeans. For daytime, it is worn with a tweed jacket and the simpler style of sporran. At a full-dress grand ball or reception, the men are splendid in velvet silver-buttoned jackets, lace-trimmed shirts, and more elaborate sporrans. The kilt also is worn as regimental dress in such Highland army units as the Argyll and Sutherland Highlanders. Lowland regiments such as the Royal Scots wear tartan trousers, which are called *trews*. (The answer to "What does a Scotsman wear under a kilt?" is: short black pants, also called trews.) Women do not wear the kilt, except for Highland dancing. Although they may wear pleated tartan skirts, these are not the same as the complicated—and very bulky—male garment.

Today, although they are a peaceable people, hospitable to all foreigners—even their ancient enemy, the English—the Scots remember their fiercer Highland heritage. Even many who are not descended from the original clans remember that heritage just as fervently. There are still "gatherings of the clans"—which were once calls to arms—in Scotland and wherever people of Scots descent have settled. There again, the old toast will ring out: "Here's tae us. . ."

A view of the island of Mull from the seaside town of Oban

A typical area in the Highlands

The Highlands
and Islands

The Lowlands

The Border
Country

Chapter 2

BENS, GLENS, LOCHS, AND ISLES

If you look at the map, you will see that Scotland has a most interesting shape; it looks like a witch. In the far north is her pointed hat and witchlike face; lower down is her cloak flying out behind. You can also see that the west coast has many, many inlets from the Atlantic Ocean and that there are a great number of islands. In fact, any map that fits on a normal-sized page cannot possibly show all 780 islands. They come in all sizes. Many are tiny and uninhabited, being too bleak and storm battered to sustain human life. Some are quite famous: Harris (where the tweed comes from), the Shetlands (where the ponies come from), Fair Isle (which is part of the Shetlands and where the beautifully patterned sweaters come from), and Skye (where Bonnie Prince Charlie escaped to after the Battle of Culloden).

You can see, too, that there are hills and mountains in most parts of the country. The mountains are mostly called *bens;* the valleys are called *glens* if they are narrow and *straths* if they are wide. Even in the cities of Scotland, one catches glimpses of nearby hills, and many of the streets themselves are built on steep inclines.

Scotland is, of course, a very small country. It is only 274 miles (441 kilometers) long, although the coastline is so jagged that it adds up to more than 2,000 miles (3,218 kilometers). At the widest point, the land is only 154 miles (248 kilometers) wide; at the narrowest, only about 25 miles (40 kilometers). Because of Scotland's narrowness and its deep inlets, it is never possible to get too far from the sea, and fishing towns and villages abound. The sea to the west and north is the Atlantic Ocean; to the east, the North Sea.

GETTING AROUND

As Scotland is such a small country, it might seem that it would be easy to drive around it in no time at all. That is not so. While there are major roadways, in order to get to some of the most beautiful spots, one has to drive on narrow, twisting roads, sometimes with room for only one car. On such roads there are frequent little lay-bys to allow one car to pull off to let another go by. The rule is that the car nearer the lay-by pulls off, backing up if necessary. Smiles and waves to indicate "please" and "thank you" are very politely exchanged.

Another thing that can slow things down on such roads is coming round one of the bends and finding oneself facing several sheep who think they have more right to the road than do the motorists. They are not a bit afraid of cars and are not nearly as good-natured as the motorists about getting out of the way.

These difficulties occur only in remote parts, however, and

Abbotsford, the home of Sir Walter Scott (left), and the ruins of Melrose Abbey (right)

there is plenty of transportation — buses, trains, steamboats — to most regions. In some areas, such as the Highlands and islands, however, it doesn't do to be in too much of a hurry. The people there like to take things calmly and leisurely.

THE BORDER COUNTRY

Approaching Scotland from England, visitors will find themselves in the Border Country. The border between the two countries is just 60 miles (97 kilometers) long and is defined by the Cheviot Hills and the river Tweed.

The beautiful farmland and rolling countryside found here were once the scene of bitter bloodshed, first with the Romans and then with the English. Evidence of many struggles can be seen in the ruined castles and abbeys. Near the abbey at Melrose is Abbotsford, the home of Sir Walter Scott, who immortalized — and romanticized — the history of the area in his Waverley novels, written in the nineteenth century. The beautiful river Tweed flows past Abbotsford, from which can also be seen the Moorfoots and

Rolling hills in the Border Country

Lammermuirs, a twin range of hills dividing the Border Country from the Lothian area. (One of Scott's novels was called *The Bride of Lammermoor*.)

THE LOWLANDS

The area north of the Border Country is called the Lowlands, although the countryside is far from flat. It is just less mountainous than the Highlands farther north. This is the most densely populated part of Scotland. It includes, to the east, the Lothian region, where the capital city of Edinburgh stands on the Firth of Forth. This great estuary (which is the meaning of *firth*) is spanned by two bridges: the modern suspension bridge for road traffic and the cantilevered railway bridge, over a mile (1.6 kilometers) long, which was the wonder of its time when it was built in the 1890s at a cost of the then-colossal sum of more than 3,000,000 pounds. The Pentland Hills provide Edinburgh with a splendid background.

Left: Loch Lomond, with Ben Lomond in the background
Right: Railroad bridge over the Firth of Forth

The city of Glasgow lies to the west, not far upriver from the Firth of Clyde. It was on the banks of the river Clyde that the great ships of the Cunard line were built, including the *Queen Mary,* the *Queen Elizabeth,* and the *QE2,* as the second *Queen Elizabeth* is known. This is the heart of the most industrial area of Scotland; yet, as everywhere else in this country, there is lovely scenery. Not too far from Glasgow is Loch Lomond. You may have heard the song about its "bonnie, bonnie banks." Above its eastern shore rises the imposing Ben Lomond or "beacon mountain." But people from the Glasgow area do not even have to go to Ben Lomond to see a mountain prospect. The Campsie Fells can be seen from many parts of the city. In fact, they are more often looked at from afar than approached, as they are of rather forbidding gray rock.

Another beautiful nearby area is that of the Firth of Clyde, with its promontories and islands. A popular place for vacationers, the scenery is delightful, the waters are good for sailing, and the resorts have remained unspoiled. One of the most popular islands

The cottage in Ayrshire where Robert Burns was born

is Arran. The boats going over there can be filled with people, but somehow all those people seem to disappear when they land — into the hills or among the small resort towns — so that no place on the island ever seems too crowded.

On the coast, across from Arran, lies the countryside from which Robert Burns came. Seeing this pleasant land, it is hard to imagine that, in his day, Burns had to toil to try to scrape a living from his tiny farm.

THE HIGHLANDS AND ISLANDS

Going still farther north, one comes into the Highlands. It is obvious why this is the name of the region, for it is almost three quarters mountainous. In this region stands Ben Nevis, "the mountain of snows," which, at 4,406 feet (1,343 meters), is the highest mountain in the whole of Britain. Other spectacular mountains are to be found in the towering Cairngorm range of

A group of hikers in the Highlands

the Grampians. Here flock hikers of great stamina and avid
mountaineers. A ski resort at nearby Aviemore attracts people in
winter.

As well as the rugged mountain areas, this region encompasses
rich farmlands and beautiful wooded glens. The land surrounding
the small town of Perth, on the river Tay, is particularly verdant.

The whole region, including the islands off the west coast, is
beloved by vacationers. It is not recommended, however, for those
who just like to lie on a beach and toast themselves. (While there
are many lovely beaches, the weather is seldom very warm—
when it gets past 70 degrees Fahrenheit [21 degrees Celsius],
people begin to mutter about heat waves—and the water is often
more than a little chilly.) People whose idea of good swimming
water is a heated pool won't enjoy the Scottish sea. For those who
like to hike, climb hills or mountains, cycle, fish, take boat trips,

Since the fourteenth century people have claimed a monster lives in Loch Ness. At left is a representation of the Monster.

or just gaze at beautiful scenery, no place is more exciting.

The major cities here are Aberdeen at the mouth of the river Dee; Dundee, at the mouth of the Tay; and Inverness, which is near Loch Ness. You probably have heard of the Loch Ness Monster. Does it or does it not exist in the unfathomable depths of this longest and deepest of all the Scottish lochs? There have been many serious attempts to find out whether some dinosaurlike beast lives here and many more claims of having seen its coils pop up in mid-loch. If anyone wants to believe that the Loch Ness Monster exists, certainly none of the local people are going to discourage the idea.

It is in the Highland region that the royal family of Great Britain has its summer residence in Balmoral Castle. It is here, in Braemar, that the famous Highland Games are held. It is here, too, that forty members of the Clan MacDonald were slain in the Pass of Glen Coe in 1692 by a company of troops from the Clan Campbell on orders of the British government. The MacDonald chief had failed to swear allegiance to the British king within the set time period. To this day, there are some Scots who hold that

Left: Many waterfalls can be found in the north of Scotland.
Right: The island of Mull lies off the west coast.

one should never trust a Campbell.

It is also in the Highland region, in the small town of Kirriemuir, that J.M. Barrie was born. Barrie is the man who gave the world *Peter Pan.*

Off the west coast is the famous island of Skye, together with others less well known outside Scotland, islands with intriguing names like Iona, Rhum, Eigg, Muck, Mull, and Coll. These Western Isles, or Hebrides, which vary greatly in size and which may have rich vegetation or be of barren rock, afford some of Scotland's most beautiful vistas as they emerge from a misty sea or are radiantly lit by the setting sun.

THE FAR NORTH

Moving into Scotland's most northerly part, one finds more mountains, with sea lochs, towering cliffs, giant waterfalls, steep glens, and stretches of moorland. The counties of Wester Ross and East Ross are rich in vegetation. In Wester Ross, warmed by the Gulf Stream from the Caribbean, even some subtropical plants flourish. As one goes farther north to Sutherland and Caithness, however, the countryside becomes starker, with spectacular rock formations and remnants of ancient Bronze and Iron Age civilizations still to be found. Both archaeologists and bird-watchers revel in this part of the country.

The far north is Scotland's most sparsely populated region. Some places are described in guidebooks as "a handful of cottages," with the number of inhabitants too small to be worth mentioning. The largest town, Thurso, in Caithness, has a population of only nine thousand. The most northerly town in Scotland, its name derives from *Thor's-a,* meaning "river of the god Thor." In this area there is still plenty of evidence of the Viking presence in Scotland from the tenth to the fifteenth centuries. The county of Sutherland gets its name from the fact that, to the Vikings, who landed first in the Orkney Islands and Caithness, it was "the south land."

THE ISLES

When people refer to the whole length of Great Britain, they say, "from Land's End to John o'Groats." Land's End is in Cornwall, at the southernmost point of England, and John o'Groats is on the northeastern tip of Caithness, the tip of the witch's hat. From John o'Groats, one can see the Orkneys, a cluster of islands that, with the Shetlands, were once a stronghold of the Vikings. The Orkneys did not become part of Scotland until the fifteenth century. These islands, even now, hardly consider themselves part of mainstream Scotland. People on the Orkneys refer to the mainland as "the Sooth," and the Norse influence is everywhere apparent.

In the Orkneys, ferries run from the harbor town of Stromness to the mainland.

The Shetland Isles are on the same line of latitude as the southern tip of Greenland and Siberia, but they are spared the Arctic weather by the Gulf Stream. They do have to suffer terrible gales, though, and no trees survive. There are magnificent fishing waters, and, as few places are more than a mile from the sea, it is hardly surprising that most of the people earn their living by fishing.

Off the west coast of this northern region lie more Western Isles, the Outer Hebrides. *Hebrides* is another word derived from Norse—*haf bred eyr,* or "islands on the edge of the ocean." On the Outer Hebrides one will certainly hear people speaking Gaelic, even the small community of Pakistanis on the island of Lewis. Most of the Outer Hebridean islands are treeless, but many have wonderful wild flowers. Barra, known as "the Garden of the Hebrides," has over one thousand varieties.

All these islanders are a very special breed. They are friendly and polite, but definitely feel that they are different from, and possibly a little smarter than, the folk on the mainland.

Above: Skara Brae prehistoric village on the Orkneys was exposed by a storm in 1851. Right: Celtic crosses, early Christian symbols, can be seen in various parts of Scotland.

Chapter 3

CALEDONIA, STERN
AND WILD

Scotland's history is long, violent, and often tragic. Reminders of it are everywhere: in the castles and buildings; in the writings of its poets; in the songs written to commemorate deeds of valor or treachery; in the tunes played on the bagpipes. Much of it has been embroidered by legend.

ANCIENT TIMES

The first recorded mention of Scotland occurs in the writings of the Roman historian Tacitus in the first century A.D. For anything that happened before that, we rely on what archaeologists have been able to deduce: the first inhabitants were nomadic hunters and food gatherers. Next, about 3000 B.C., came Neolithic immigrants who farmed, were weavers and potters, and also were builders of stone structures, including *cairns*, circular burial chambers whose remains still can be seen today.

Remains can also be seen of the Bronze Age people of about 2000 B.C. On the island of Lewis, there is a great circle of standing stones, together with a group of cairns, which is certainly religious in meaning and which is one of the most important

Hadrian's Wall

relics of the Bronze Age in the whole of Britain. Remains of the Iron Age people of about 500 B.C. are to be seen in *brochs,* which were fortified towers. There are different theories about where these various people came from, and historians do not always agree.

What Tacitus had to report was the invasion of what is now southern Scotland by the Roman Ninth Legion, led by the Roman governor of Britain, Gnaeus Julius Agricola. (The Romans called this territory *Caledonia,* a name that is still sometimes used for Scotland in literature and that is preserved in names such as the Caledonian Canal. There are also Caledonian societies for Scots abroad.) Agricola defeated the Caledonians in the Battle of Mons Graupius in A.D. 83. For some unknown reason, he was ordered to withdraw in the following year, and the Romans were never again to win a decisive victory in this part of the world. In the 120s, the emperor Hadrian built a wall from the river Solway to the river Tyne in northern England (most of which can still be seen), and

*A carved stone
left by the Picts
on the Island of Raasay
in the Highlands*

twenty years later the Antonine Wall (little of which remains) was
built from the mouth of the river Clyde to the mouth of the river
Forth. The idea seems to have been to contain the Caledonians
rather than to conquer them. In 208 the emperor Severus ventured
as far north as the Moray Firth but met with constant guerrilla
resistance from which he soon retreated. Soon after, the Romans
retired behind Hadrian's Wall and made no further attempt to
make Caledonia part of the Roman Empire.

FROM ALBA TO SCOTIA

By the fifth century, Scotland consisted of four different
peoples—the Picts, the Scots, the Britons, and the Angles—who
would eventually merge to form the kingdom of Scotland. The
largest group, the Picts, of European Celtic stock, occupied the
land from the far north to the river Forth. In the Strathclyde area
were the Britons (also Celts), who had been driven from England

*Iona Cathedral is built on the original
site of St. Columba's monastery on Iona.*

by invading Angles and Saxons. To the east of them were some of
those Anglo-Saxons. In what is now Argyll, Kintyre, and the
Western Isles was the kingdom of Dalriada, inhabited by the Scots,
a Celtic race from northern Ireland. The country was then known
as Alba or Alban. The process of unification was slow and
bloodstained.

Dalriada long maintained its ties with Ireland, and it was from
Ireland that Columba (later made a saint) came to found a
Christian mission on the island of Iona in 563. The Briton Ninian
(also later made a saint) had, some two hundred years earlier, led
missions to other parts of Alba, but his influence was limited.
Columba, who interested himself in politics as well as religion,
was to go farther afield (he is said to have encountered a monster
at Loch Ness) and succeeded in establishing an organized church.
Iona has remained a religious center throughout the centuries. St.
Oran's Chapel, built in 1080 on what is believed to have been the
site of St. Columba's original chapel, still stands. Its cemetery is
the oldest Christian burial place in Scotland, and fifty kings are
buried there, including the famous Macbeth about whom
Shakespeare wrote.

From the ninth to the fourteenth centuries, the Norwegian

Vikings descended on Scotland, eventually putting an end to Pictish domination of the north. In 843, Kenneth MacAlpin, king of the Scots of Dalriada, took advantage of the weakness of the Picts and declared himself king of all territory north of the river Forth. His realm became known as Scotia. (This name is also often used poetically and survives in the name Nova Scotia.) Thus the Picts faded into obscurity, and today historians are not even sure where they originally came from or how they came to be called Picts. Some say that the name was given to them by the Romans because they painted themselves. (The Latin for "painted" is *pictus*—the same root from which we get the word *picture.)*

SCOTLAND TAKES SHAPE

Almost two hundred years after Kenneth MacAlpin, the rest of what is now mainland Scotland was added to the domain of Duncan I. This is the Duncan who figures in Shakespeare's *Macbeth.* In 1040 Duncan was killed by Macbeth in battle—not murdered, as in the play. Macbeth, who succeeded to the throne, was in fact a wise king who brought Scotland seventeen years of prosperity. Macbeth was killed by Malcolm, Duncan's son, which is one way in which history matches the play.

Malcolm became King Malcolm III and married Margaret, an English princess who had fled to Scotland to escape the Norman Conquest in 1066. During their reign, these two introduced many English influences to Scotland, attempting, for one thing, to make the church conform to the English pattern. On behalf of his wife's family, Malcolm periodically tangled with the Normans in the north of England. He was killed in an ambush during one of those border raids in 1093.

King Malcolm III

For the next thirty years, Scotland was misruled by a series of weak kings and it wasn't until 1124 that a measure of stability returned with the accession of David I, ninth son of Malcolm. David, brought up in England and with many Norman friends, married a rich Norman heiress and held, through her, the title of Earl of Northampton and Huntington. He later annexed Northumbria in the north of England. Thus David was a powerful figure in both Scotland and England. Under his rule, the Norman influence in Scotland became very strong. He attempted to establish a national system of justice, and his reign was largely peaceful.

BEGINNING THE AULD ALLIANCE

On David's death, his successor was Malcolm IV, an eleven-year-old boy. Many times in Scotland's history, the accession of a child monarch—some much younger than eleven—left Scotland prey to warring factions. Among those causing trouble for young

William the Lion

Malcolm was Henry II of England, who forced him to return Northumbria to England. When Malcolm died at the age of twenty-three, his brother, William the Lion, angry at the loss of Northumbria, formed an alliance with France and attempted to invade England. Although he was defeated and forced to place Scotland under feudal subjection to England, the connection with France—which became known as the Auld Alliance—endured for centuries. In 1189 William was able to buy back Scotland's independence from the English king, Richard the Lion-Hearted, who was then raising money to go on a crusade.

For a century there was peace between Scotland and England but not, alas, peace in Scotland. The chieftains of the southwest repeatedly defied the central monarchy and attacked Anglo-Norman strongholds. The Lords of Lorne in the west and the Lords of the Isles off the west coast considered themselves independent or, if owing allegiance to anyone, loyal to the kings of Norway. These kings, too, laid claim to much of Scotland. It was only after a defeat at the battle of Largs in 1263 that the

Balliol surrenders to Edward I   *Alexander III*

Norwegians gave up the Hebrides (the Western Isles). Twenty years later, following the marriage of the daughter of Alexander III, grandson of William the Lion, to King Eric of Norway, the two countries made a permanent peace.

Upon Alexander III's death in 1286, his heir was his grandchild Margaret, the infant daughter of the King of Norway. Edward I of England proposed that this child be married to his son and that Scotland would then be independent, except for English garrisons in the south. Although the Scots did not care for this idea, it never became an issue; the little queen died on her way over from Norway.

Several rivals claimed the Scottish throne, the two strongest being Robert Bruce and John Balliol. Edward I stepped forward, offering to support Balliol in return for his promise of loyalty and subjection, including help in Edward's proposed invasion of France. Balliol, instead, revived the alliance between Scotland and France and invaded England. Edward seized the excuse to invade Scotland, where many of the nobles, including Robert Bruce,

Left: A statue of Robert Bruce
Right: William Wallace's army on
its way to fight Edward I

actually welcomed him. However, having defeated Balliol, Edward continued to rampage through Scotland, taking many towns and castles and forcing many nobles to do him homage. The final indignity came when he captured the ancient Stone of Destiny, or Stone of Scone (pronounced scoon), the traditional stone on which Scottish kings had been crowned for seven centuries. (It remained in Westminster Abbey in London, undisturbed until a party of Scottish Nationalists daringly whisked it away in 1950—much to the delight of the Scots.) It seemed that Edward, known as the Hammer of the Scots, had subdued Scotland.

SCOTS WHA HAE

In 1297 there arose one of Scotland's great heroes—William Wallace. In that year at Stirling Bridge, at the head of an army of resistance from all parts of Scotland, Wallace wiped out a large part of the English army. The next year Wallace was defeated by an army led by Edward I himself, and in 1305 he was captured and executed in London. Scottish resistance did not, however, die with him.

A statue of Robert the Bruce at Stirling Castle

The next national hero to emerge was Robert the Bruce, son of the man who had been Balliol's rival. This Bruce had himself crowned Robert I at Scone in 1306. Defeated by the army sent to quell him, he became an outlaw. (There is a legend that when he was in despair, lying hiding in a cave one day, he watched a spider trying again and again to spin a thread from one corner to another. Supposedly, Bruce was so impressed by the spider's refusal to give up that he determined that he, too, would try again—to defeat the English.)

Bruce went back into action, gathering around him many of the powerful Scottish nobles and harassing the English army in guerrilla warfare. Edward I, setting out to punish this rebel, died en route. Edward II, of weaker fiber than his father, left the English garrisons to fend for themselves and, by 1314, Bruce had driven the English from every town except Stirling. Edward II finally decided to lead an army against Bruce. This army was soundly defeated at Bannockburn, near Stirling, and the English fled across the border. For the next fourteen years, skirmishes between Scots and English took place in the north of England, not on Scottish soil. In 1328 a peace treaty recognized Scotland's independence, and Bruce's four-year-old son was married to Joan, little sister of the English king, Edward III.

Robert Burns wrote a poem, "Bruce's Address to His Army at Bannockburn," commemorating the two great heroes. The poem begins:

Scots wha hae wi' (who have with) Wallace bled;
Scots, wham (whom)Bruce has often led;
Welcome to your gory bed,
Or to victory!

and ends with this stanza:

Lay the proud usurpers low!
Tyrants fall in every foe!
Liberty's in every blow!
Let us do, or die!

This poem has been set to music and is still sung when Scots are in a particularly patriotic mood.

ENTER THE STUARTS

By 1329 Robert the Bruce was dead, and his successor was five-year-old David II. A regent—someone who rules in place of a monarch—was appointed, and once more Scotland was at the mercy of warring factions. With Scotland in a state of chaos, again the English stepped in to take over the Lowlands. The boy king and his wife were sent to France for safety, and the regency passed to Robert Stewart, son of Bruce's daughter, Margery. With the help of the French, Robert Stewart drove the English out of most

James IV of Scotland

of their strongholds, and the young king was able to return to Scotland.

By this time the English were entangled in the Hundred Years' War with France, and the Franco-Scottish alliance went into full swing. When the English were engaged with France, the Scots could have a breathing space; and when the French wanted the Scots to harry the English, they in turn obliged. On one of these forays, David was captured and sent to the court of Edward III, where he spent twelve years. Far from finding his captivity a hardship, David enjoyed it very much. Although he was ultimately returned to Scotland after payment of a huge ransom, the Scots did not particularly want him back nor did he want to be back. He returned to England and tried to declare Edward's younger son his heir.

The Scots were having none of that. On David's death in 1371, Robert Stewart, the former regent, was crowned king — the first monarch in the long line of Stewarts. (The spelling of the name was later changed to Stuart.) Neither this first Stewart king nor his son, Robert III, could control the quarreling noble families, however. Robert III's son, who was to become James I, was sent to

France for safety but was captured at sea by the English and, after his father's death, spent the first eighteen years of his reign as an English hostage.

It was not till 1424 that James was able to return to Scotland. He immediately took steps to subdue the rebellious nobles. James renewed the alliance with France—sending a Scottish contingent to fight with Joan of Arc against the English—and introduced many social and legal reforms in Scotland. His strong measures naturally earned him many powerful enemies and three of them, including his uncle and cousin, stabbed him to death in 1437.

Once again Scotland had a boy king—six-year-old James II. And again the warring nobles went uncontrolled. It was not until 1455 that James was able to restore a semblance of order. Five years later James II was killed by a bursting cannon at the siege of Roxburgh, where he had gone to support Henry IV in the Wars of the Roses.

The new king was another child—nine-year-old James III. This meant another regency and more strife, which continued even after James himself took over. In fact he had to imprison his own two brothers, who were leagued against him. A group of conspirators seized James's young son and proclaimed him king. While attempting to fight these rebels, James was thrown from his horse and was stabbed to death as he lay waiting for help.

James IV, fifteen years old when he came to the throne, was the most popular of the Stewarts. Learning and the arts, peace and prosperity came to the land. Great churches were built and towns and trade flourished. The first printing press was established in Edinburgh in 1507. James was able to control the rebellious nobles of the Lowlands. He also attempted to make friends with the clan chiefs of the Highlands and islands, although without much success. In 1502 he signed a treaty of perpetual peace with England and, in the next year, married Margaret Tudor, the young daughter of Henry VII. It was this marriage that eventually united the two kingdoms.

Although James IV sincerely wanted to live in peace, he was drawn into war with England through the Auld Alliance with France. He, and others who were considered to be "the flower of Scottish chivalry," were slain at Flodden Field in the north of England in 1513. This tragedy is memorialized in a lament, "The Flowers of the Forest Are A' Wede (all withered) Away." This song is still played on the bagpipes and is guaranteed to bring tears to the eyes of the listener.

The new king was again a baby, his mother was a Tudor with no great allegiance to Scotland, and intrigue was again rife, while Henry VIII menaced Scotland from the south. James V, by the time he was fourteen and supposed to be governing, was a prisoner of the powerful Douglas family. He escaped from them two years later and tried to restore peace. This was the time when Martin Luther's call for reformation of the Catholic church had all Europe in turmoil. Scotland, as a factor in the balance of power, was courted by Henry VIII, who wanted her to join him in Protestantism and turn against France. When James resisted, Henry sent troops to Scotland in 1542. James, in ill health, attempted a counter-invasion of England but died just as the news was brought to him that his daughter had been born. "It came with a lass and it will gang with a lass," he said before he died. He was referring to the fact that the Stuart line had attained the throne through Margery Bruce and was prophesying that it would die with his daughter. In this he was quite wrong.

Mary, Queen of Scots

THE ROMANTIC MARY

The daughter was Mary, Queen of Scots, one of the most romantic figures of history, about whom books, plays, poems, and even an opera have been written. She was a week old when she became queen, and the inevitable intrigue began all over again. Henry VIII sought to betroth her to his young son, but her mother, a Frenchwoman, was not about to let that happen. She rejected the treaty of marriage that had been agreed to by the regent. Henry's answer was to send troops to Scotland to burn and pillage Edinburgh and the Border Country. This devastation and bloodshed was known as the Rough Wooing.

Mary, when she was six years old, was sent to France to be betrothed to the Dauphin, the king's son. By this time, religious strife had increased. The leaders of the Catholic church in Scotland had long been rich and corrupt, and the ideas of reformation, spreading from Europe, were welcomed in Scotland. In 1544 we first hear of John Knox, the fiery preacher who was to

John Knox

John Knox's house in Edinburgh

establish Protestantism in Scotland and to become a fierce enemy of Mary. In 1557 the First Covenant, renouncing the Catholic church, was drawn up by a group of Scottish nobles.

In 1558 Mary married the Dauphin, who became king of France the following year. In the meantime, John Knox triumphed. He introduced measures to abolish all traces of Roman Catholic ceremonies from the Scottish church: the keeping of Christmas and Easter were abolished; Holy Communion was seldom celebrated; and social, as well as religious rules, were set by the Kirk Sessions, the head body of the Church of Scotland. There was an atmosphere of grim austerity in the land.

Mary returned to this scene, widowed at eighteen. Not only was she beautiful and high-spirited, but she was a Catholic—a figure unwelcome to the stern church leaders. Mary made a point of not thrusting her religion on her people and surrounded herself with Protestant nobles. However, there was no way she could please the Kirk Sessions. She proceeded to scandalize them by marrying her high-living young Catholic cousin, Lord Darnley. He became jealous of Mary's Italian secretary, David Rizzio, whom he helped

Lord Darnley

Mary, Queen of Scots,
bidding farewell to her subjects

murder. Then Darnley, in his turn, was strangled—no one knew by whom. The chief suspect was the Earl of Bothwell and, a few weeks after Darnley's death, Mary caused more scandal by marrying Bothwell. Even though he was a Protestant, Mary was not forgiven for marrying him.

In 1567, when she was just twenty-four, Mary was captured by a group of Protestant nobles, paraded in disgrace through the streets of Edinburgh, and forced to abdicate in favor of her one-year-old son, James—Darnley's son. Once more, Scotland had an infant king, James VI. Mary tried to regain power but was defeated and fled to England, where she threw herself on the mercy of her cousin, Queen Elizabeth. Elizabeth, however, was under great pressure from her ministers to have Mary executed. The English queen imprisoned Mary, eventually accusing her of conspiracy. Mary, Queen of Scots, was beheaded in 1587. The two queens never met, and it is often suggested that Elizabeth was not only afraid of Mary's claim to the English throne but was also jealous of her beauty and charm.

Ruins of Urquhart, one of the largest castles in Scotland. It was blown up in 1692 to keep the Jacobites from using it. The Jacobites were Scotsmen loyal to James VII, a Stuart king.

Chapter 4

THE UNITED KINGDOM

THE BEGINNINGS OF GREAT BRITAIN

After Mary was deposed, Scotland was once more ruled by
regents, and young James VI, already harshly treated by the tutor
who raised him, was fought over by rival nobles and finally
kidnapped by a Protestant group. In 1583 he escaped and assumed
the throne. In spite of his frightening childhood, James grew up to
be a stable character who tried to rule wisely and who, although
remaining a Protestant, did not oppress the Catholics. He had
great trouble, however, with the ruling officials—called the
Presbytery—of the Scottish church who tried to intrude
themselves into the government of the country.

In 1603 came the great change. Elizabeth died. James, as her
heir, became James I of England, as well as James VI of Scotland.
He went to London. It was a union of crowns but not yet of
kingdoms, although James referred to the two countries as Great
Britain. James's most lasting legacy is the King James version of
the Bible. The one used in most Protestant churches, this
translation of the Bible is renowned for the beauty of its language.
Since James authorized its translation, it is dedicated to him.

Greyfriars Church, where the National Covenant was signed

CIVIL WAR IN ENGLAND

James was succeeded in 1625 by his son, Charles I, who antagonized his Scottish subjects by trying to impose the forms and ideas of Episcopalianism, the English version of Protestantism. Charles's attempt to introduce the prayer book of the Church of England into the Scottish religious service caused a riot in Edinburgh, followed by widespread protests and the signing of a new National Covenant. Support for the Covenant led to open warfare and, to combat Scottish attacks, Charles was forced to summon the English Parliament to grant him funds. He had not convened Parliament for more than ten years, believing that he governed by "divine right of kings." Once summoned, Parliament seized the chance to oppose Charles, to execute his favorites, and, eventually, to embark on a civil war against the king in 1642. The two sides were known as Cavaliers, for the king, and Roundheads, for Parliament.

Left: Oliver Cromwell at Marston Moor
Right: The execution of Charles I

The Scots Covenanters—as the supporters of those who had signed the National Covenant were called—joined with the parliamentary forces under Oliver Cromwell to defeat the Cavaliers at Marston Moor in 1644. Of course, as the Scots had not agreed among themselves for centuries, there was a faction that fought for the king and harried the Covenanters for two years before being finally defeated. Charles surrendered to the Covenanters, who handed him over to Cromwell, hoping that Cromwell would help establish Presbyterianism in England. They found that he was going to do no such thing. One faction thought they might be better off with the king, after all, and sent an army into England to restore him to the throne. They were severely defeated, and those who had not agreed with the idea of rescuing the king welcomed Cromwell to Edinburgh. A few days after Cromwell returned to England, Charles I was executed.

The Scots did not like this at all; Charles had been their king, too, and of Scottish descent. They proclaimed his son Charles king and brought him to Edinburgh in 1650. Cromwell immediately invaded Scotland. The Scots were routed and Charles escaped to Europe.

THE GROWTH OF UNION

Cromwell garrisoned Scotland with English troops, setting up a firm central government and formally uniting the two countries in a Treaty of Union. By all accounts, this union was to Scotland's advantage in that it brought peace and economic benefits. That didn't mean that the Scots were at all grateful, for they had lost their independence.

When Cromwell died and Charles II was restored to the throne, he governed Scotland through a Privy Council in Edinburgh and a Secretary in London, but never again visited Scotland himself. Charles tried again to establish Episcopalianism in Scotland. Many ministers refused to accept this and left their churches, conducting services in the open air or in barns. Before long, fighting had broken out between the Covenanters and government forces.

In 1685 Charles died and was succeeded by his brother, James II, who was a Catholic. Although James was willing to extend religious tolerance to his subjects, they were not willing to extend it to him. Before long, his son-in-law, William of Orange, a Dutchman, was invited to assume the throne, and James fled to France.

Many in Scotland—especially in the Highlands—did not want this Dutch usurper. They wanted their rightful Stuart king. These Jacobites, as they were called, sprang to arms and remained a source of trouble for years. While relations between Scotland and England continued to be bad, there was growing in Scotland a feeling that they would need to seek peace for the sake of trade and prosperity.

When William died in 1702, he was succeeded by his sister-in-law Anne, who did not produce a living heir. The English feared a

Stuart restoration. James Edward Stuart, son of James VII and a Catholic, was waiting in the wings. The English offered the crown to a German princess, Sophia of Hanover. In 1707, after much negotiation, the Scots agreed to a union of parliaments and to a Hanoverian succession in return for commercial equality with England. They were to retain their own legal system and the Presbyterian form of religion. Scottish members of Parliament were greatly outnumbered by the English—a condition that still exists today. The Jacobites responded to the situation with a song that says, "We were bought and sold / for English gold."

"THE KING OVER THE WATER"

There remained in Scotland much opposition to the union of parliaments, and the Jacobites, in particular, did not abandon hope of restoring their Stuart king. "The king over the water" was a popular toast that can still sometimes be heard even today. By this time George I of Hanover was on the throne. He was not liked in either Scotland or England. In 1715 James Edward called the Scottish clans to support him. He was proclaimed king in Scotland. Thousands of clansmen rallied round him and, at first, it looked as if they might be victorious. As usual, the great families of Scotland were not united, and the rising was defeated by Scot fighting Scot. In the aftermath, many Jacobites were shipped to plantations in America, and an attempt was made to disarm the clansmen and stamp out the use of Gaelic.

The Jacobite cause continued to simmer. Few in Scotland loved the new king, George II, who ascended the throne in 1727, and England was at war with Spain and France. It seemed that the Jacobites might have European allies. Also, they had a worthy

Bonnie Prince Charlie's headquarters was the only building to survive the Battle of Culloden.

figure to lead them—Prince Charles Edward, a young, handsome, charming man—Bonnie Prince Charlie. In 1744 Prince Charles set sail for the Hebrides from France.

CHARLIE'S YEAR

At first Charles's reception was not too warm, but gradually he was joined by some three thousand clansmen. They reached Edinburgh, where Charles's father, James Edward, was again proclaimed king. Charles installed himself in Holyroodhouse Palace. He defeated government forces at nearby Prestonpans and, a few weeks later, crossed the border, bent on reaching London. He got within 110 miles (177 kilometers) of the capital but was persuaded, against his will, to withdraw to the Highlands to raise more troops. Scotland was, as ever, divided, and by the time Charles set up headquarters in Inverness, many clans had joined the Hanoverian side. By the spring of 1746, a large, well-equipped army had been assembled in Aberdeen, commanded by the Duke of Cumberland, the English king's son.

Left: A monument commemorating the Battle of Culloden Moor
Right: Prince Charlie's farewell to Flora Macdonald

There followed the tragic Battle of Culloden Moor, where Charles's ragged and hungry Highlanders were slaughtered by the English cavalry. Charles escaped and, for months, was hunted with a price of 30,000 pounds on his head. Although that was an immense sum to people of that day and those parts, no one betrayed him. His escape to the island of Skye is one of Scotland's favorite stories. Disguised as a maidservant, he was rowed across the sea by a young woman named Flora Macdonald. There is, of course, a song about it:

> Fly bonnie boat, like a bird on the wing
> > Over the sea to Skye.
> Carry the lad who was born to be king
> > Over the sea to Skye.

Charles had spent just fourteen months in Scotland—a period known as "Charlie's Year." He spent the rest of his life as an unhappy exile in Europe but has lived on in memory along with Mary, Queen of Scots, as one of the two great romantic figures of Scottish history.

THE DESTRUCTION OF THE CLANS

The English revenge for the uprising was cruel. Scores of people were slaughtered; the Highland countryside was devastated; houses were burned and cattle driven away. Again, hundreds of Scots were shipped to plantations and a determined effort was made to destroy the clan system. Tartans and bagpipes were banned, and no one was allowed to bear arms.

The breaking up of the clans resulted in the notorious Highland Clearances, which continued for almost a century. As the clan system shriveled, the chiefs lost the old sense of responsibility for those who lived on their land. Many of these landlords, or *lairds*, drove their tenants—whom they no longer needed for their private armies—off the land, often burning their houses and turning the land over to sheep grazing. In fact, this is why one still sees so many sheep in the Highlands today.

Thousands emigrated and others flocked to the cities to become cogs in the machinery of the Industrial Revolution. Many were recruited into Highland regiments, which fought gallantly all over the world for the Hanoverian royalty that had treated them so badly.

A GRADUAL MENDING

Slowly the wounds began to heal. The restrictions on Highland dress and bagpipe playing were withdrawn and estates were returned to their owners. With the end of fighting on Scottish soil, trade could be developed. In the second half of the eighteenth century and the beginning of the nineteenth, literature and the arts flourished as never before, particularly in Edinburgh. The

Prince Albert and Queen Victoria

poet Robert Burns and the novelist and poet Sir Walter Scott were not only part of this flourishing, but, by their writings about Scotland and their use of the Scottish dialect, they helped build up Scottish morale. They presented to the rest of the world what we would now call "a good image."

The image presented was so good that, in 1822, George IV made a state visit to Scotland, clad in Royal Stuart tartan and eager to make himself pleasant. Later, Queen Victoria became a true enthusiast. Her beloved consort, Prince Albert, helped design Balmoral Castle, where British royalty has gone ever since for part of the summer.

In the Victorian era, Scots played a large part in maintaining the British Empire overseas. Because the Scottish educational system produced more talented people than Scotland itself could provide with jobs (a situation that still remains), many went abroad as engineers, civil servants, merchants, missionaries, and explorers. The most famous of the explorers was David Livingstone who was reported missing in Africa. He was finally found in the jungle by

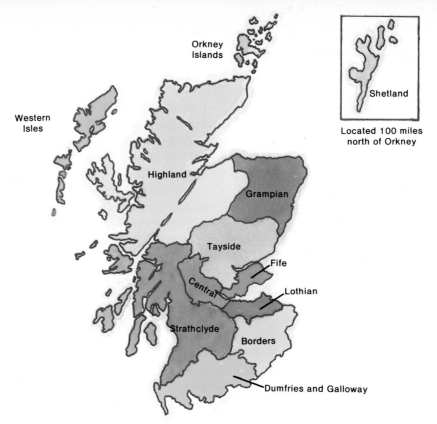

Orkney Islands

Shetland

Located 100 miles
north of Orkney

Western Isles

Highland

Grampian

Tayside

Fife

Central

Lothian

Strathclyde

Borders

Dumfries and Galloway

the American newspaperman, H.M. Stanley, who greeted him
with the now celebrated words, "Dr. Livingstone, I presume?"

The Scots retain not only a strong feeling of independence from
the rest of Great Britain, but they also have a marked difference in
local government and in their judicial and educational systems. In
London there is a Scottish Office, headed by the Secretary of State
for Scotland, who is appointed by the prime minister and has a
seat in the British cabinet. Most of the actual administration of the
Scottish Office is carried out from Edinburgh.

Scotland is now divided, for local government purposes, into
regions: Dumfries and Galloway; the Borders; Strathclyde,
Lothian, and Central; Fife; Tayside; Grampian; Highland;
Western Isles; Orkney; and Shetland. These regions embrace the
various *shires* (counties), such as Lanark, Argyll, Aberdeen, and so
on. Local people still use these shire names.

In general elections in Britain, Scots have often voted against the

Ramsay MacDonald was the first prime minister of Britain from the Labour party.

mainstream. In the past, they tended to favor the Liberal party over the Conservatives, and Socialism has always been popular in Scotland. The first British prime minister to belong to the Labour party was Ramsay MacDonald, who was born in the little Highland village of Lossiemouth.

Between the two world wars, Glasgow and its environs was known as the "Red Clydeside" because so many people supported the independent Labour party, which was further to the left in its ideas than the official Labour party. Scotland suffered great economic distress in the Depression, which made the ruling Conservative party in England even more unpopular. In the recent 1983 election, very few Scots voted for Margaret Thatcher's Conservative party, and the fairly new Social Democrat party did better in Scotland than in many other parts of Britain.

In 1934 the Scottish National party was formed. Its members believe that Scotland should be completely independent of the rest of Britain. Others hold that Scotland should remain connected but that laws particularly affecting the country should be dealt with by a special legislative body in Scotland. However, when in 1979 an opportunity was given to the Scots to vote on this home rule, or "devolution," not enough electors turned out to get the necessary majority for the plan to be accepted.

Princes Street in Edinburgh has a magnificent landscaped sunken garden.

Chapter 5

THE HISTORIC PRESENT

The largest cities in Scotland are Glasgow, Edinburgh, Aberdeen, and Dundee. These four cities are special in that their mayors are called Lord Provosts, rather than just provosts as in other towns.

EDINBURGH—THE ATHENS OF THE NORTH

Edinburgh has been the capital of Scotland since the middle of the fifteenth century. Its Scottish Gaelic name, *Dunneideann*, means "hill fort of Eiden." Edinburgh is commonly thought to be one of the most beautiful of all European cities and is frequently compared with Athens. Edinburgh is not highly industrialized— being, rather, a financial center—although brewing, distilling, and printing have been carried on there for centuries and new industries in electronics and nucleonics have been developed. It is the city, above all, that visitors to Scotland want to see, for here history is a living presence.

Edinburgh's main street is Princes Street, which is surely

Edinburgh Castle, built on an extinct volcano, overlooks the city.

unique. On one side are various stores such as one would find in any big city. On the other side lies a beautiful sunken garden beyond which, standing on a huge volcanic rock, is the magnificent Edinburgh Castle.

Edinburgh Castle was built in the eleventh century and was added to at various times. A chapel built in 1075 for Queen Margaret, wife of Malcolm III, is still in use. Every day, except Sunday, a "one-o'clock gun" is fired from the castle grounds. When the castle is floodlit at night, it floats against the blackness of sky and rock like a real castle-in-the-air.

Down from the east side of the castle slopes the Royal Mile, which ends at the Palace of Holyroodhouse. First used as a residence by James IV in the sixteenth century, the palace was lived in for a few years by Mary, Queen of Scots. Visitors can see her suite of rooms in the northwest corner tower and the tiny

The Old Town of Edinburgh, with St. Giles Cathedral (right) in the background

room where her son James was born. They can also see a brass plate, which is said to be set on the very spot where her secretary Rizzio was stabbed to death. Bonnie Prince Charlie also stayed at Holyroodhouse briefly. Today there is a suite set aside for the present queen when she visits Edinburgh. Close by Holyroodhouse is Holyrood Park and Arthur's Seat, a craggy hill that looks somewhat like a resting lion. Anyone who climbs its 822 feet (251 meters) will be rewarded with a beautiful view of Edinburgh.

The castle and the Royal Mile are in Edinburgh's Old Town, where there are many other historic buildings. There is St. Giles Cathedral, the High Kirk (church) of Edinburgh where John Knox preached. Nearby is the tiny house where he lived. In this small area of Old Town are packed the tenements—sometimes up to fourteen stories high— where once all the people of Edinburgh lived huddled together. One of those buildings is known as Brodie's Close. In the eighteenth century a Deacon William Brodie lived there. He was a town councillor by day and a burglar by night. It was from his life that Robert Louis Stevenson got the idea for *The Strange Case of Dr. Jekyll and Mr. Hyde.*

Princes Street and the area behind it are part of New Town, which was begun in 1767 as an extension to the city. Here are beautiful Georgian houses and squares, including St. Andrews Square, one of the wealthiest squares in the world. Leading banks and insurance companies have their headquarters here, although the stately buildings look too refined to be dealing in anything as ordinary as money.

New Town was the center for the literary life of eighteenth-century Scotland. Dr. Samuel Johnson, an Englishman who compiled the first dictionary, visited here with his biographer, James Boswell. (Johnson was very nasty about Scotland. He said that the fairest prospect a Scot could see was the road to England. But then, Johnson was well known for his acid tongue.) Robert Burns was a celebrity here for a while, and Sir Walter Scott lived here. Edinburgh was so proud of Sir Walter Scott that, in 1844, the city erected a 200-foot (61-meter) monument to him that is a landmark on Princes Street.

Edinburgh has expanded much beyond both its Old and New Towns and has buildings of all periods. Somehow, however, the character of the city has not been spoiled. One of its charms is that there are rural areas within the city limits. Dean Village and Cramond Village are two picturesque little sections that take visitors completely by surprise.

But then, Edinburgh is full of surprises. For instance, it has a statue to a dog, Greyfriars Bobby, a little terrier that, after its

Above left: One of the most popular shopping streets in Edinburgh is Princes Street. In the left foreground is the Scott Memorial built in 1844. Other interesting sights are a horse-drawn beer wagon (top right), the Antarctic penguins parading in the Edinburgh Zoo (above), and quiet spots such as White Horse Close (left), which originally was a terminal for horse-drawn coaches.

Above: A view of Edinburgh from Edinburgh Castle. Below: During the late summer the Military Tattoo, a spectacle of military bands, bagpipers, and drums, is performed on the castle esplanade.

*The floral clock
in Princes Street gardens*

shepherd master died in 1858, stayed by his grave in Greyfriars Cemetery till its own death in 1872. And in the Edinburgh Zoo, there is one of the largest colonies of Antarctic penguins in captivity. Each day, weather permitting, they march out in the famous and delightful Penguin Parade. Another Edinburgh surprise not to be missed is a floral clock in Princes Street Gardens. This clock, which measures 11 feet 10 inches (361 centimeters) in diameter, is set in the ground. Its face and hands are completely covered with a variety of some 24,000 flowers and plants. And it actually works. The large and small hands go round and a cuckoo pops out every quarter of an hour.

Edinburgh is a fascinating city at any time of the year, but it is even more wonderful for three weeks in August and September, when the International Festival comes to town. This festival, which started in 1947, brings concerts, plays, poetry readings, art exhibits, ballet—every kind of performance. Many works are performed here for the first time. Perhaps the most popular of all events for visitors from abroad is the Military Tattoo, which is held on the castle esplanade. Thousands every year thrill to the sight and sound of splendidly kilted pipers and drummers as they march on the floodlit parade ground.

One of the most important streets in Glasgow is Sauchiehall Street.

GLASGOW—THE FLOURISHING CITY

Just a short train ride west from Edinburgh is Glasgow, whose name means "green glen." The city's motto is "Let Glasgow Flourish," which is suitable for a city that is at the center of Scotland's busiest commercial and industrial area. Glasgow first began to flourish in the seventeenth century, when it began to trade with America and when the river Clyde, on which it stands, was widened and deepened so that ocean-going vessels could sail right into the center of the city.

Iron and steel industries and engineering companies attracted thousands of people to Glasgow in the nineteenth century—particularly Highlanders dispossessed by the Highland Clearances and Irish fleeing famine and poverty in their own country. Before World War II, the population of the city had reached more than 1,000,000. But in recent years, almost 200,000 people have been

The Glasgow Art Galleries

relocated to nearby new towns built to relieve the congestion and to rehouse people from what were some terrible slums.

There is a rivalry between Edinburgh and Glasgow. Edinburgh is inclined to think that people from Glasgow (who are called Glaswegians) are rather rough in their ways. Glasgow is inclined to think that people from Edinburgh put on airs. Edinburgh likes to think it is superior in culture, but Glasgow won't agree with that. After all, Glasgow has the older university and it has the Scottish National Orchestra, the Scottish Opera, and some of the best art collections in all of Europe. Glasgow has always been a great theater town, too, and its own Glasgow Citizens Theater has been a training ground for the whole country.

Certainly Glasgow does not have as many elegant areas as Edinburgh, but it does have some of the finest examples of Victorian architecture to be found anywhere, and the Glasgow School of Art, designed by the famous architect Charles Rennie Mackintosh, is a superb Art Nouveau building. It was built in 1897-99 and was much ahead of its time.

The Glasgow Cathedral was begun in 1238. In the foreground is the Necropolis, a Victorian cemetery with pillars and temples.

In recent years there has been much cleaning of buildings, and many that were once grim and gray have emerged in the lovely pale rose color of the sandstone of which they are constructed. There are more than seventy public parks in the city, with flowers everywhere, including George Square, where the City Chambers, the council meeting place, stands. Many attractive riverside walks have also been created.

Glasgow is, above all, a lively town. Its people like to enjoy themselves and are particularly fond of dancing—from the traditional Scottish dances to disco. It is a friendly town, known for its tolerance, which is undoubtedly why so many people from India and Pakistan are settled here quite happily. They, of course, have picked up the local accent, which is quite distinctive. In fact, anyone who has learned that Glasgow is pronounced "GLAZ-goh" may be taken aback slightly to hear Glaswegians calling it "GLESS-cah."

An old saying tells us that "The Clyde made Glasgow and Glasgow made the Clyde," but the decline of shipbuilding in recent years has brought changes to the area. More people are engaged in service industries now than in manufacturing. More cargo from abroad is handled farther downriver than formerly. But as the center of the British National Oil Corporation and the home of the Offshore Supplies Office, Glasgow is getting its share of Scotland's oil prosperity. And, however uncertain the future of almost all industrial areas today, Glasgow has confidence in its ability to adapt and to flourish as it has in the past.

Glasgow has its own unofficial song, "I Belong to Glasgow," which was popularized by an entertainer called Will Fyffe, who, funnily enough, came from Dundee.

ABERDEEN—THE GRANITE CITY

Aberdeen is known as the granite city because so many of its buildings are built of the local granite, a sparkling white stone that gives the city a clean, fresh look. Aberdeen has a clean, fresh smell, too, as it is set at the mouth of the river Dee, from which position its name comes—*Aber,* meaning "mouth of," and *deen,* "of the Dee." It is the third largest fishing port in Great Britain.

Aberdeen has been a fishing port since the ninth century, and now it is an oil town, too, taking part in the North Sea oil boom. The city grew from two separate *burghs* (boroughs)—Old Aberdeen, where the ancient cathedral and university are, and New Aberdeen, which is really equally old. The entire city was burned in 1337 by Edward III but was rebuilt on a grander scale. St. Machar's Cathedral was founded in 1136, but the one seen today dates from after the fire. The oldest part of the university is

The bustling port of Aberdeen

King's College, named for James IV and established in 1494. In New Aberdeen stands Mareschal College, which was established in 1593 to provide a Protestant college as an alternative to the Catholic King's College.

Aberdeen has a splendid art gallery, a children's museum, and an exciting Gordon Highlanders' Museum with banners, uniforms, and weapons from that famous regiment, founded in 1794. Aberdeen has two special festivals. Every August, for two weeks, it holds the International Festival of Youth Orchestras and Performing Arts, and every June, the Aberdeen Festival has nine days of Highland games, dancing, and pipe music.

DUNDEE—CAKE, MARMALADE, AND MUCH MORE

Dundee stands at the mouth of the Tay, Scotland's longest river (120 miles-193 kilometers). It is a busy seaport and another of the towns to benefit from the oil boom. Industrial success is not new to this city, as it carried on a brisk wool trade in the seventeenth century and was the center of the Scottish linen industry in the

Dundee

eighteenth century. Then in the nineteenth century Dundee became the chief importer of jute from India and the world center for the spinning and weaving of flax.

Before it settled into prosperity, however, Dundee had more than its share of destruction. It was sacked by the English in 1296 and again in 1385. It was a center of fighting in the English civil war and was occupied by the Jacobites before the Battle of Culloden. As a result, there are very few old historical relics to be seen—just the Old Steeple of the eleventh-century town church and a sixteenth-century town gate called Wishart Arch.

Although it is such a busy city, Dundee provides plenty of green space for its residents to enjoy. There are twenty-eight parks and four golf courses. And Dundee *is* busy. Apart from being a port and being in the oil business, it also produces whiskey, carpets, and the two items that have been enjoyed around the world—Dundee marmalade and Dundee cake, the latter a delicious, very rich fruitcake thickly topped with almonds.

The river Ness flows through the city of Inverness.

INVERNESS—CAPITAL OF THE HIGHLANDS

Inverness is another of those Scottish towns with a castle on one of the main streets. The one there now was built in the nineteenth century—although there was an earlier one built in the twelfth century. The present castle is built on the site of Macbeth's stronghold, which was blown up by Bonnie Prince Charlie.

Inverness is a port, with its own fishing fleet, and is also a railway junction for trains to the west and north. It is at the head of the great Caledonian Canal, which runs in an almost direct diagonal southwest to the opposite coast. The strange thing about this remarkable waterway is that it is a man-made canal only for about one third of its 60 miles (97 kilometers). The rest of the way, it links up natural lochs. In summer, from Inverness, visitors can take a boat trip through the first part of the canal out into Loch Ness (keeping a keen eye out for the monster, of course). Just a short bus or automobile ride from Inverness is Culloden Moor, where that last, fateful battle was fought.

The Fair Maid's House in Perth is supposedly the house that is featured in Sir Walter Scott's novel The Fair Maid of Perth.

PERTH—GATEWAY TO THE HIGHLANDS

Perth is a charming little town that was once the capital of Scotland. Nearby is Scone Palace, where the Scottish kings used to be crowned. The palace that stands today is not the original, but a nineteenth-century structure. It houses a museum of porcelain and embroidery, including a tapestry worked by Mary, Queen of Scots.

Perth today is a market center for the surrounding farms and, standing as it does on the river Tay, is also an inland port, as it has been since the thirteenth century. The stormy waves of history often swept through Perth. It was here that James I was assassinated. The town's once lovely monasteries were destroyed in response to the passions stirred up by John Knox, who launched the Protestant Reformation in Scotland from St. John's Kirk here. Walter Scott wrote a novel called *The Fair Maid of Perth* and the house in which the heroine is supposed to have lived still stands.

The club house at St. Andrews Royal and Ancient Golf Club

OTHER INTERESTING TOWNS

Stirling, in central Scotland, has a magnificent castle that towers over the city. There is also a huge monument to William Wallace, which can be seen for miles around. Bannockburn, the scene of Robert the Bruce's famous victory, is near here. Stirling, too, has a festival in the spring.

Then there is St. Andrews on the east coast, which has two claims to fame. It has the oldest Scottish university, founded in 1410, and the Royal and Ancient Golf Club, which was founded in 1754. The latter is the most famous golf course in the world, and many championship games have been played here.

Dunfermline, in the east central region, was also once the capital of Scotland. (One of the most famous anonymous Scottish ballads, "Sir Patrick Spens," begins, "The king sits in Dunfermline town / Drinking the blude-red wine.") Robert the Bruce was buried in its now-ruined abbey in 1320. Andrew Carnegie, who made his fortune in America, was born here in 1835.

Ayrshire with Ailsa Craig in the distance

Ayr is situated on the coast southwest of Glasgow. Its principal industry is sometimes said to be Robert Burns, as so many mementoes of him are sold there. The cottage in which he was born is only two miles (three kilometers) away at Alloway. Burns, of course, had something to say about the town: "Auld Ayr, whom ne'er a town surpasses / For honest lads and bonnie lasses."

Farther south on the coast are the ruins of Turnberry Castle, which was the childhood home of Robert the Bruce. Most people who go to Turnberry nowadays, however, don't go for that reason; they go to play on its splendid golf course. Near here, too, standing amid beautiful gardens and woodlands, is Culzean Castle. This magnificent building was designed by Robert Adam in the late eighteenth century. After World War II, an apartment in Culzean Castle was made available to Dwight D. Eisenhower in gratitude for his achievements as the American commander-in-chief who coordinated the Atlantic Forces in World War II.

Across the sea from this area can be seen the strange, onion-shaped, 1,100-foot-high (335-meter) rock that is the island of Ailsa Craig, on which stands a famous lighthouse. The lighthouse is known as "Paddy's Milestone" because so many Irish immigrants sailed past it on their way to find work in the city of Glasgow.

Left: The harbor town of Portree is the capital of Skye.
Right: A farmer's house on Skye

The lure of seeing where Bonnie Prince Charlie hid out draws many people to the island of Skye. But even without its romantic background, Skye would be worth visiting for its dramatic scenery. In its center are the 3,000-foot-high (914-meter) Cuillin Hills, and its coastline has hundreds of sea lochs and bays. Visitors are also attracted by Skye's archaeological past (the Norse ruled the island until the thirteenth century) and by its tartans and tweeds. Fifty miles (80 kilometers) long and 25 miles (40 kilometers) wide, this most beautiful of all the Scottish isles is renowned for the quality of its light and air. Although thousands of tourists go there each year they are not allowed to spoil the charm of the place.

If you visit the island of Jura, you will be seeing the place where George Orwell wrote his famous novel *1984*.

To describe all of the many enchanting places to visit in Scotland would require an entire guidebook. Most of them still bear evidence of the country's stormy history, which is one of the reasons why the Scots are so aware of how the past has shaped the present.

Chapter 6

LIVING AND LEARNING

Life in Scotland, for many people, has often been hard. In the early days, constant warfare kept large parts of the country poor; in more recent years there has often been widespread unemployment. Even today, many Scots have to go abroad, as there are not enough jobs for the high percentage of well-educated people produced by the schools and universities. (According to statistics for 1980-81, 24 percent of young people go to a university in Scotland, while only 13.6 do in England.) Because living was often hard, many Scots had to be very careful with their scarce money. There is a phrase, the *canny* (cautious) Scot, which means that Scots are cautious, not only about money but also about life in general. But it was their care with money that gave rise to jokes about Scots being skinflints—jokes that were often made by Scots comedians themselves. However, nobody who has ever been to Scotland and enjoyed the hospitality there puts much stock in the outworn jokes.

Today most Scots live comfortably, many are prosperous, but few live in real luxury. A too lavish style of life—even for those who could afford it—would not be considered proper. How do these Scots, some 5,000,000 of them, make their livings? As in all developed countries, there are the usual professional people and those engaged in service jobs. About 35 percent are employed in manufacturing.

INDUSTRY

The pattern of industry has changed in recent years. Shipbuilding and coal and steel production have declined, but electronics and light engineering have developed. The hydroelectric industry thrives and is carefully controlled by the Northern Hydro-Electricity Board so that the various dams do not spoil the scenery or the environment. Particularly in the remotest parts of the north, this board has brought not only electricity but also social and economic improvement, greatly changing the lives of those who had struggled for centuries with harsh living conditions.

The most exciting industrial development has been the discovery of oil in the North Sea. This has given employment to thousands, both those engaged directly in extracting the oil and those supplying all the subsidiary needs of the industry.

In the coastal areas, many make their living by fishing. Fishermen catch such hauls as herring, haddock, cod, sole, crab, and lobster. They often brave extremely stormy seas. Women, too, are vital to this industry; many of them, known as fishwives, clean the fish as the catches arrive in the harbor.

Farmers grow such crops as oats, barley, wheat, potatoes, and fruit. The richest farmland is in the Central Lowlands; the poorest is in the Highlands, where the farms are just tiny *crofts*—small

Left: Utility ships from the North Sea oil production in the harbor of Aberdeen. Right: Sheep are found all over Scotland.

pieces of land worked by tenant farmers—and most of the land is used to graze sheep.

Because of all those sheep, Scotland developed a famous wool trade. Probably the best-known product is Harris tweed, which is spun, dyed, and hand woven on the islands of Harris, Lewis, Uist, and Barra—all part of the Hebrides. This tweed is very strongly made and lasts for years and years, which is why it is used for making very classic suits, jackets, and coats. Classic styles remain in fashion year after year, regardless of trends, so people do not tire of a style while the fabric is still in excellent condition. Also, like wine, tweed is considered to be best when aged. More than 7,000,000 yards (6,400,800 meters) of Harris tweed are produced each year.

There are many less bulky wool fabrics produced in small towns like Hawick, in the Border Country, and Pitlochry, in Central Scotland. These fabrics are woven in various patterns

A potter from Dunvegan, Skye (left), and Tartan blankets

including, of course, the many tartans. Also much knitting wool (do not call it yarn) is produced in subtle colors that are blends of several shades; the loveliest capture the true colors of nature, such as heather or moss.

Knitting wool is also made into sweaters (the Scots call them *jumpers*), the most famous of which are the Fair Isle patterned ones. Handknit in wool spun from the sheep that are bred on the Shetland Isles, these sweaters use delicately colored designs, closely related to those found in Norwegian sweaters (remember, this was once Viking territory).

There are many craftspeople working in Scotland today. Some produce silverwork that uses old Celtic or Viking designs or thistle patterns, the thistle being the Scottish national emblem. Others work in pottery or glass.

One of the industries for which Scotland is most renowned is the production of whiskey, or as the rest of the world calls it, Scotch. When the Scots say whiskey, they mean only the kind they produce. The word comes from the Gaelic phrase *uisge beatha* (pronounced, roughly, "us quay bach"), which means "water of life." The finest type is malt whiskey, made only in the Highlands from an extract of malted barley that has been dried over a peat

Thistle, the Scottish national emblem

Harvesting barley

fire, which gives it a unique, smoky taste. It is aged in oak casks for up to fifteen years and is the most expensive type. There are also grain whiskey, made from maize, barley, or oats, and blended whiskey, which is a mixture of grain and malt whiskeys. The Scots shake their heads in disapproval at those who put water or — horror of horrors — ice in whiskey. But they know that, of the more than 40 million gallons (151,500,000 liters) exported each year, a lot is going to be diluted that way.

RELIGION

The principal religion in Scotland is Presbyterianism, and the official church is the Church of Scotland. Each year in Edinburgh, a gathering of ministers and elders of the church meets, not only to discuss church affairs but also to give its views on many matters affecting the life of the country and of the world in general. The Lord High Commissioner represents the queen on those occasions, and sometimes she herself will attend. Once the church had great influence on all Scottish affairs and, indeed, many of the battles fought in the old days were fought in the name of religion.

There was a time, too, in Victorian and Edwardian days, when the Scots Presbyterian church was a most repressive factor in Scottish life. The Sabbath, as Sunday was called, was a very gloomy day. Church twice a day, with Bible class and Sunday school for young people, was the rule. No work could be done and Sunday newspapers were considered sinful. In particularly extreme households, window shades were drawn all day. And on any day of the week such pastimes as dancing were frowned on— which is probably why so many people learned to love to dance! Such narrow ways are long gone, and churchgoing has declined steeply in recent years. But definite traces of the old Scottish Sabbath remain. In many places, absolutely no shops and very few restaurants are open on Sundays and excursion trips do not operate. This can all be very upsetting to tourists who do not know what to expect.

There are many Roman Catholics in Scotland, many descended from the Irish who came to Scotland to find work. Although the days of actual religious warfare are long gone, there are two soccer teams in Glasgow—the (Protestant) Rangers and the (Catholic) Celtics—whose supporters have been known to come to blows, especially over the match played every New Year's Day. Innocent visitors from abroad have to be assured that this is just a ritual, and that the participants are actually enjoying themselves!

There is complete freedom of religious choice in Scotland today and a full range of religious beliefs—although the Scots are not naturally inclined to get involved in any of the more unusual cults that flourish in some parts of the world.

LAW

The Scottish legal system is based on Roman civil law, which means that court decisions derive from legislation. The English and American system, on the other hand, is based on common law, which derives from custom and precedents established by former cases. Marriage laws are less strict in Scotland than in England, and it is possible for young people to get married in Scotland without parental consent. Until 1856 it was possible to get married in Scotland simply by stating one's intent before two witnesses. This practice led to a great trade in such marriages in Gretna Green, a little village in Dumfries just across the Scottish border. Couples from England used to elope there to be married in front of the anvil by the village blacksmith. In fact, even after the marriages had to be more formal, couples continued to elope to Gretna Green because it was the romantic thing to do.

Another major difference in Scottish law is that the courts, in criminal cases, allow not only a "guilty" or "not guilty" verdict, but also a "not proven." This means that if there is real doubt as to the accused's guilt or innocence, the jury need not, against its better judgment, choose one or the other definite verdict. Also the jury—which consists of fifteen, rather than twelve people—need not reach a unanimous verdict; a majority vote is sufficient.

EDUCATION

Education in Scotland has always been more democratic than in England. Scotland does not have the equivalent of public (really private) schools like England's Eton and Harrow. There are few private schools, and of these hardly any are boarding schools. The

St. Andrews, Scotland's oldest university

most famous one is Gordonstoun, which was attended for a time by Prince Philip, Duke of Edinburgh and husband of Queen Elizabeth, and by Charles, Prince of Wales. This school is renowned for its strict program and for teaching the boys to "rough it."

All Scottish children must attend school from age five to sixteen. Some, especially those planning to attend a university, will stay longer. The Scottish Education Board supervises the schools, together with local education authorities. Although separate vocational and academic schools are permitted, the trend, particularly in urban areas, is toward comprehensive schools that offer both choices.

The Scots have always held education in high esteem and have encouraged their children to study to get ahead, often making sacrifices to send children on for higher education. Entrance to

Left: Glasgow University, designed by Sir George Gilbert Scott
Right: Heriot School, founded in 1628

Scottish universities is based firmly on academic achievement, with provision for poor but bright students to get financial help from a variety of scholarships. Andrew Carnegie, who made his fortune in America, left millions to help Scottish students. Although those who attend universities can manage, if they are so inclined, to have a full social life, they are expected to work hard; and there are no trivial courses offered.

Scotland has eight universities—ranging in age from Aberdeen, Glasgow, and St. Andrews, all founded in the fifteenth century, to the University of Strathclyde, founded in 1963 (when it encompassed the much older Royal Technical College). The others are Edinburgh, Dundee, Stirling, and Heriot-Watt. Edinburgh has one of the world's most respected medical schools. Other important educational institutions are the Glasgow School of Art and Napier College for adult education in Edinburgh.

*Top: Seafood is plentiful in Scotland.
Left: Scottish food is usually
hearty and hot.
Middle: Children
in a playground in Glasgow
Bottom: A couple
dancing at a ceilidh accompanied
by an accordion*

Chapter 7

SCOTTISH SPECIALTIES

Because of the strict rules that the Presbyterian church imposed on everyday life, the Scots had a reputation for being very solemn. But there were always plenty who reacted against the gloom of the *unco guid* (the super-good). The Scots, on the whole, are a cheerful people, although their straight-faced brand of humor often escapes other people, who do not always realize that jokes are intended. As in all nations, types vary, and there are those who do take life very seriously. They are usually called *dour* (DOO•er) Scots.

But the majority of Scots like to enjoy themselves in many ways. They watch television, of course—either the BBC (British Broadcasting Corporation) or Independent Broadcasting Authority. The BBC has a Scottish regional branch that contributes some radio and TV programs of special local interest. Many of the most popular American programs are also shown.

There are plenty of filmgoers and many enthusiastic theater patrons. Apart from regular theaters in the cities, there are many little theaters that blossom in the summer. For instance, there is a beautiful Festival Theater in Pitlochry, an attractive village set in

Fiddle and accordion players

almost the exact center of the country. People come from all over to attend it. (Pitlochry has been a popular resort ever since Queen Victoria's doctor said its air was the healthiest in all Scotland.) The smallest professional theater is in a converted barn on the little island of Mull.

DANCING AND MUSIC

A great many people of all ages love to dance. Of the traditional dances, the eightsome reel, danced by eight people, is most often performed. It is danced quite wildly, to the accompaniment of loud cheerful cries—except when it is being very formally danced, in which case the dancers are quiet and dignified. Two other old favorites are the Highland fling and the sword dance. The latter is danced in the sections created by two crossed swords. These traditional dances are most fun when danced to bagpipe music, which is called "little music" when it is played for marching and dancing and "big music" when it is played as warlike music and laments, or *pibrochs.* Bagpipes were often used by Highland regiments going into battle to inspire the troops and scare the

Performing the Highland fling (left), and Scottish pipers

enemy. The latest historic occasion when they were used in this way was at the Battle of El Alamein in World War II, which was fought in the North African desert. The wailing sound (it is called the *skirl*) of the pipes had a particularly weird effect, as the pipers could not be seen through the swirling sand.

Pipe bands have been formed in most areas of the world where large numbers of Scots have settled, and the famous Black Watch band has regularly played abroad to enthusiastic crowds in such places as Madison Square Garden in New York. One of the most thrilling sounds, however, is to hear a lone piper in the hills in the dusk of a summer evening, with the music floating across a beautiful Scottish loch.

In addition to the bagpipe music, Scotland has a rich treasury of songs, as anyone who likes folk music will know. Records by such singers as Ewan McColl, Jeanie Ritchie, and Jean Redpath have carried these songs around the world.

The Scots invented the game of golf in the twelfth century.

Bagpipe music and Scottish dancing are an important part of the Highland games, which are held in various parts of Scotland and abroad. The most famous of these events is the Royal Highland Gathering at Braemar in the Grampian region. The royal family usually attends. Events include putting the shot—throwing a very heavy round stone as far as possible—and tossing the caber—heaving end-over-top the huge trunk of a fir tree, which is over 19 feet (6 meters) long and 120 pounds (54 kilograms) in weight.

SPORTING LIFE

Scotland's most famous game is golf, which was invented there in the twelfth century. There are plenty of inexpensive public courses, so that anyone interested can afford to play. Many of these courses are very scenic, as they often run along the coastline. A great number are quite hilly, so there is a lot of strenuous walking to be done. Sheep are often allowed to graze on the courses to keep the putting greens cropped.

Scotland's favorite spectator sport is soccer—or football, as it is called in Britain. Glasgow is particularly football mad. The

Lawn bowling

Football Association was formed there in 1873 and by the 1890s there were thirty-five clubs in the city. Before World War I, the first stadium in the world to hold a crowd of 100,000 was built at Glasgow's Hampden Park. There are many amateur teams, and soccer is played at most schools. Some rugby football, or rugger, is played, but it has not captured the hearts of the people the way soccer has. Although many of the soccer players become very famous and play in international matches, they do not earn the enormous sums that American football players do. As soccer depends on fast moving and skill in maneuvering a ball, the players do not need to be large and husky, with the result that some of the best players do not look the part of the traditional athlete.

Many people play lawn bowls in which large, carefully balanced bowling balls are rolled across a "green" toward a small, white target ball, called the jack. The game is much like the *bocce* ball that Italians play. A similar game, called curling, is played on ice. Instead of balls, the players use round, flat, polished granite stones. Each curler has a long-handled broom that is used to sweep *(soop)* in front of the stone to keep the ice free of obstacles as the stone moves toward the house (goal).

Shinty, *a type of field hockey, is played in the north.*

There is a type of no-holds-barred field hockey, called *shinty*, that is played in the north. Shinty has been described as the fastest game in the world and one has to be brave to play it, as it can get very rough. The Irish play a similar game called *hurley*.

The Scots are great walkers and have plenty of beautiful country to explore. Many also enjoy climbing hills and mountains. Scotland also offers sites for skiing and sailing, plus lovely roads for cycling. There is marvelous fishing along the coast or in the streams and lochs. There is hunting of deer, grouse, and pheasant, but this is always on private land and is available only to the few who can afford it—although, of course, there are always a few poachers! The hunting of deer is called deerstalking, and the type of hat that used to be worn—like Sherlock Holmes's—is called a deerstalker.

NEW YEAR AND OTHER FESTIVITIES

The most important holiday in Scotland is New Year. The festivities begin with *Hogmanay,* which is New Year's Eve. After midnight, people go "first footing," which means they go visiting friends and the first one to step over someone's doorway in the brand-new year is the "first foot." It is considered most lucky if the first foot is a dark-haired man bringing a gift. It used to be thought that a lump of coal was the luckiest gift, but people today bring cake or whiskey. The merrymaking usually goes on far into the night, with people going from house to house. More visiting takes place the next day. Scots will never wish anyone "Happy New Year" until the last stroke of midnight has sounded. It is considered bad luck to say it before then, but people continue to say it throughout the month of January if meeting each other for the first time in the new year.

Burns Night, honoring the beloved poet, is celebrated on January 25. On November 30 some Scots celebrate St. Andrew's Day. St. Andrew was the patron saint of Scotland when the country was Catholic. There are St. Andrew's societies, as well as Burns societies, all over the world. The old flag of Scotland is a diagonal white cross of St. Andrew on a dark blue background. This is one of the flags incorporated into Britain's Union Jack. There is also a Royal Scottish standard—red lions on yellow background.

Among other festivities are very special gatherings called *ceilidhs* (CAY • lies) traditionally held in small rural or island communities. People come from miles around to drink, eat enormous quantities of homemade food, dance, and sing—old and young together. *Ceilidhs* usually go on all night.

FOOD APLENTY

The most world-famous Scottish food is *haggis*, which is traditionally eaten on Burns Night. The recipe for haggis doesn't sound too appealing: it consists of the heart, liver, and lungs of a sheep or calf ground up and mixed with suet, onion, oatmeal, and seasonings and then all boiled together in a bag made from a sheep's stomach. Yuk! you might well say. Lots of people love it and it is much tastier than it sounds—or looks—but, it is not really an everyday food.

One of the haggis ingredients, oatmeal, is the meal ground from oats, not the hot cereal that you may have eaten. (That cereal, in Scotland, is called porridge.) Oatmeal is often used instead of flour or bread crumbs to coat fish. It is also used to make oatcakes, a thick usually triangular, type of cracker most often eaten at breakfast.

Some Scots eat their main meal in the middle of the day and then will have high tea at 5:30 or 6 o'clock. High tea includes a cooked course such as sausages, fish and chips (french-fried potatoes), or even bacon and eggs. Besides this there will be a selection of breads and what the Scots call tea bread—sweet rolls, scones, crumpets—and perhaps a cake or little fancy cakes, called *gateaux*, or French cakes. Gateaux are frosted, are filled with whipped cream, or are chocolate covered. Most often, such cakes are served only when there is company or as a weekend treat. When it's just family, there will usually just be a "plain" tea.

About that teabread: scones are what Americans call biscuits, and the word is pronounced "scawns," not "scoons" as in Scone Palace. Crumpets are very thin pancakes that are buttered and rolled up like miniature jelly rolls. They are wonderful eaten hot,

A butcher shop in Fort William

but watch out for dripping butter! (In England, crumpets are like English muffins.)

Another teatime treat is shortbread, which is made of sugar, butter, and flour, baked either in large rounds or small bars. It is very crunchy and rich and definitely not for dieters. You may have tasted a so-called shortbread cookie, but these are much thinner and not nearly so buttery as the true shortbread.

Some households will have afternoon tea at 4 o'clock and dinner or supper at 7 or 7:30. Afternoon tea is like high tea, minus the cooked course. The Scots drink a lot of tea, not only with meals but at any time they feel in need of a lift. "A wee cuppa tea" is a cure for a lot of ills.

A lot of mutton is eaten in Scotland—naturally, with all those sheep—and there is very fine beef, especially from the Aberdeen Angus cattle. Scottish potatoes, tomatoes, and strawberries are all very fine. But the country does not rely only on home produce. The food in the stores comes from near and far, particularly from the European Economic Community, of which Great Britain is a member.

Fresh salmon being hung in a smokehouse

One thing that Scotland certainly does not need to import is fish. It is plentiful and always very fresh because it never has to be transported very far. Herring are very popular. They are eaten at either breakfast or high tea and are best coated in oatmeal. They are also smoked—over peat fires, just like the best malt whiskey—and then become kippers. Kippers have a very special smoky taste and are delicious—if one likes strong-tasting food. Another especially good fish is finnan haddie—smoked haddock—which is named for the little Highland town of Findon where the smoking process was developed.

The most delicious fish of all is salmon, which is of superb quality and is often flown to expensive restaurants overseas. It is expensive even in Scotland. Trout, which is caught in the rivers and *burns* (streams), is also a great delicacy and salmon trout, which has a pinkish flesh, is exceptionally tasty.

Soup is very popular in Scotland. Great quantities of soup are eaten in winter to insulate people from the damp cold. The mere

Red deer

smell of a simmering pot of soup is a cheering thing, and Scots prefer to make their own, tending to despise the canned variety. The most popular type is Scotch broth, which is made from mutton stock and is thick with vegetables and barley—a positive meal in itself.

VARIOUS BEASTIES

Beastie is an old Scottish word for "animal," and there are many animals to be found in Scotland, some of which are special Scottish breeds.

Deer abound in the Highlands. Burns, as usual, has a poem about that:

> My heart's in the Highlands, my heart is not here,
> My heart's in the Highlands, a-chasing the deer.

A special herd of some 1,500 red deer live on the island of Rhum. These deer are protected by the Nature Conservatory Council against anyone's chasing them. Other wild animals to be found in Scotland include otters, pine martens, and wildcats. Seals can be seen off the coastline in some areas. The many varieties of birds include golden eagles and falcons, and thousands of sea gulls wheel hopefully around all the fishing boats.

Highland cattle have unusual, shaggy coats.

The Scots raise famous breeds of cattle: Aberdeen Angus, which yield wonderful beef; Galloway and Ayrshire, which produce fine dairy products; and the unique Highland cattle, which are particularly hardy and easy to recognize. Highland cattle have long, shaggy, reddish coats and wide-spreading horns. They are often featured on postcards, and models of them are sold in gift stores, along with model Loch Ness Monsters.

Scotland claims two special breeds of horse: the sturdy Shetland pony and the enormous Clydesdale. The latter is now mainly seen at shows and ceremonial occasions but was originally bred as a particularly strong workhorse. Clydesdales used to be employed in pulling huge cartloads of coal, barrels of beer, or other heavy materials. They are notable for their magnificent manes, tails, and leg hair and, when all decked out with silver and leather bridles and other ornaments, are a truly impressive sight.

West Highland terrier

An animal that still very much earns its keep is the Scotch collie. Not too large and with a black-and-white coat, this dog is an exceptionally clever sheep dog, superb at herding sheep together and at finding lost ones. Sheep-dog trials, at which these dogs compete with one another in displaying their skills, are held in many parts of Britain. These trials are so popular that they are often televised.

Then there are Scotch terriers—or Scotties—short-legged, rough-coated, almost square little black dogs. A whiskey manufacturer uses a black Scottie and a similar white dog as a trademark. The white variety is called a West Highland terrier. There is also a Cairn terrier, which is brownish or grayish and is built on slimmer lines than the Scottie. All these breeds, as with the Shetland pony, the Clydesdale horse, and the cattle, have been exported to and bred in other parts of the world.

Chapter 8

FAMOUS SCOTS

POETS AND NOVELISTS

The arts somehow managed to flourish in Scotland even in times of turmoil, and there is a rich heritage of poetry. The earliest poets were unknown bards whose anonymous ballads have been passed down through the centuries. The earliest known poets include William Dunbar, Robert Henryson, and John Barbour, all of whom wrote in an old Scots dialect that is very difficult to read today. Many of the nobles wrote poetry, as did two of the kings, James I and James V. Scotland also proudly claims to have produced the world's worse poet—William McGonagall, who lived in the nineteenth century and was given to celebrating the wonders of his age in lines like this:

O, wonderful city of Glasgow, with your triple
expansion engines
At the making of which your workmen may get singeins.

The most famous and best-loved poet is, of course, Robert Burns (1759-1796). He lived only thirty-seven years, most of them as a poor tenant farmer, but his poems, which made him the most popular man in his own locality in Ayrshire, brought him ultimate literary success in Edinburgh. His fame spread around the world, as the many Scots who went abroad carried his poems

Robert Burns

with them. In countless places Scots celebrate his birthday on January 25—Burns Night—with singing and bagpipe playing, poetry reading, and drinking. Nothing could be more appropriate for, above all, Robert Burns loved a party.

Burns wrote mainly in the Scots dialect and, for the most part, about ordinary things because he was writing for the ordinary people among whom he lived. One of his best-known poems is "To a Mouse," addressed to a field mouse that he startled one day when he was ploughing. "Wee, sleekit, cow'rin, tim'rous beastie," it begins, and it contains the famous lines, "The best laid schemes o' mice and men / Gang aft a-gley [go often awry]." (It is from those lines that John Steinbeck got the title for his book *Of Mice and Men*.) Many of Burns's poems have been set to music, among them "Auld Lang Syne"; "Scots, Wha Hae"; "Flow Gently, Sweet Afton"; "Ye Banks and Braes o' Bonnie Doon," and the one that many consider to be one of the loveliest of all love songs, which begins, "O, my Luve is like a red, red rose."

Sir Walter Scott (1771-1832) is the other famous literary figure in Scotland. He, like Burns, was concerned about preserving the Scottish language and traditions. He collected many old ballads from the Border Country in which he eventually settled and wrote many poems of his own celebrating historical events.

Robert Louis Stevenson (left) and Sir Walter Scott

Born and educated in Edinburgh, Scott became a lawyer and then was involved in an unsuccessful publishing and bookselling business. It was the failure of this venture that set him to writing novels to pay off his debts. And these novels were his greatest achievement. Known as the Waverley novels, they presented a highly romanticized picture of history but, at the same time, gave a true picture of the Scottish character and explained what the old ways of life had meant. Among the most famous are *Rob Roy, The Heart of Midlothian, Ivanhoe,* and *Old Mortality.*

Robert Louis Stevenson (1850-1894) was also born in Edinburgh and studied law, although he never practiced it. He developed tuberculosis early in life and left Scotland as a young man to find a better climate. Stevenson spent many years in America and eventually settled in Samoa, where he was much loved by the people who called him *Tusitala* (teller of tales). Among the books for which he is famous are *Treasure Island, Kidnapped,* and *The Strange Case of Dr. Jekyll and Mr. Hyde.* His collection of poems, *A Child's Garden of Verses*, is still popular with children.

J.M. Barrie (Sir James Matthew Barrie) (1860-1937) was born in Kirriemuir, Angus, the son of a weaver. Apart from his celebrated

J.M. Barrie

Peter Pan, or the Boy Who Wouldn't Grow Up, he wrote other well-known plays, such as *The Admirable Crichton, Mary Rose,* and *Quality Street.* He also wrote novels set in Kirriemuir, which he called Thrums. Among these is the popular *The Little Minister.*

Scotland continued to produce writers in the twentieth century. Hugh McDiarmid, a well-known poet of the first half of the century, led a movement to revive writing in Lallans (a Lowland Scots dialect). Lewis Grassic Gibbon wrote a trilogy of Scottish life called *A Scots Quair,* one novel of which was adapted as a television play, "Sunset Song." John Buchan (who later became Lord Tweedsmuir, governor-general of Canada) wrote many exciting spy novels, including *The Thirty-nine Steps* and *Greenmantle.* Compton Mackenzie was a most prolific writer of novels, essays and criticism. His books were both serious and humorous. In later life, Mackenzie settled on the island of Barra, off the west coast of Scotland, and wrote several very funny novels about Highland life, including the one that was made into the film *Tight Little Island.*

OTHER WRITERS AND SCHOLARS

John Duns Scotus was a thirteenth-century theologian who challenged many of the accepted beliefs of his day. Those who

101

David Hume (left) and James Boswell

disagreed with him began to use his name as a term meaning someone who was stupid, which is where the word *dunce* comes from—an unfortunate way to be memorialized.

David Hume, an eighteenth-century Edinburgh-born philosopher, was an influential and controversial figure whose work is still studied and debated today. *A Treatise on Human Nature* and *Essays Moral and Political* are his best-known works.

Thomas Carlyle was Scotland's most eminent historian. His three-volume history, *The French Revolution,* was published in 1837. He was also a well-known essayist. Carlyle's gifted Scottish wife, Jane Welsh, was an accomplished letter writer. Collections of her letters were first published in 1883.

It seems strange that perhaps the most famous book in economics, *The Wealth of Nations,* was written by a philosopher, Adam Smith. Professor of moral philosophy at Glasgow University in the eighteenth century, Smith was a brilliant lecturer. Among those who heard him was James Boswell.

James Boswell (Bozzy, to his friends) practiced law in Scotland but dearly loved to slip off to London whenever possible to enjoy the literary life. His *London Journal, 1762-63* is the first volume of the journal of his own life. It was also in 1763 that he met the great Dr. Johnson and began to write down his every word. Boswell's *The Life of Samuel Johnson* is one of the world's greatest biographies.

Boswell himself has a modern biographer, David Daiches, who is the most prominent literary critic in Scotland today. Daiches also has written biographies of Scott, Burns, and Stevenson. His many other writings range from the two-volume *A Critical History of English Literature* to histories of Edinburgh and Glasgow and a very popular book, *Scotch Whisky*.

FILM STARS

Scotland has contributed a few stars to the world of films. Both David Niven and Deborah Kerr were born in Scotland, as was Sean Connery, who was the first star to play a major part—James Bond—without turning his Scottish accent into an English one. Gordon Jackson, who gained widespread fame as the butler, Hudson, in the TV serial *Upstairs, Downstairs*, has been appearing in character parts in films since he was a very young man. The director Bill Forsyth, who makes films in Scotland about Scotland, has become popular with three of his films, *Gregory's Girl, Local Hero*, and *Comfort and Joy*, which have had worldwide distribution. And the most famous maker of documentary films in the 1940s was John Grierson, a Scot, whose work is still studied today in film courses.

PAINTERS AND ARCHITECTS

Scotland's first notable painters were the eighteenth-century portraitists Allan Ramsay and Sir Henry Raeburn. Raeburn was

The elegant Charlotte Square in Edinburgh was designed by Robert Adam.

particularly successful and was very popular socially. He painted such celebrities as Sir Walter Scott, James Boswell, and Adam Smith. The artist must have been very fond of his wife because, for one birthday, he built her not merely a house but an entire little street! It is called Ann Street (her name, of course) and can be seen in Edinburgh today in all its charm. Other fine painters in Scotland include Sir James Guthrie, William MacTaggart, John Pettie, and Sir David Wilkie.

Charles Rennie Mackintosh was the leader of the artistic Modern Movement in Glasgow at the turn of the century. He is best known as the architect of the Glasgow School of Art and for his advanced ideas on interior design. Mackintosh was interested in every detail—furniture, light fixtures, textiles. When he was commissioned to design two tearooms in Glasgow, he—with his wife, Margaret Macdonald, also an artist and craftswoman— designed everything right down to the teaspoons. Some of his beautiful furniture can be seen at Glasgow University, along with many of the lovely watercolors of plants and flowers that he painted in later life.

Robert Adam was a leading Scottish architect of the eighteenth century. It was he who designed Edinburgh's beautiful Charlotte

Square. He and his brother James, who was almost as much in demand, were known also for interior design. An Adam fireplace or ceiling is still a prized detail in great houses in Scotland and England. Two other Adam brothers also were accomplished architects, and all had been trained by their father. Theirs was a remarkable family.

INVENTORS AND OTHER ENTERPRISING PEOPLE

Most people do not realize how many inventions came out of Scotland, but the Scots are very proud of how much they have contributed to modern life.

You already know about Charles Macintosh and his raincoat. Macintosh came from Glasgow—where they have great cause to bless his name! Another man who put rubber to good use was Robert William Thomson of Stonehaven. He created the first tires—solid and pneumatic—in 1845 when he was just twenty-three years old. Among Thomson's other inventions were the first fountain pen and the rotary engine.

Then there is James Watt of Greenock, who developed the power of steam. It is said that he got the idea as a boy from watching the lid of a kettle bob up and down as it boiled on a fire, but obviously there was a lot more to it than that. The bicycle was invented by Kirkpatrick Macmillan, a blacksmith in Dumfries. And the tar surface used to pave roads (macadam) is named for its inventor, John McAdam of Ayr.

Alexander Graham Bell may have invented the telephone when he got to America, but the Scots will be quick to remind you that he was born in Edinburgh and attended lectures at the university there. They will also tell you that John Paul Jones, an early

American naval hero, was born in the little Scottish town of Kirkbean.

John Logie Baird, educated at the Royal Technical College and Glasgow University, was a pioneer of television. In 1926, he demonstrated, for the first time ever, the televising of moving objects. He demonstrated color TV in 1928 and was researching stereo TV when he died in 1946.

In the medical world, Sir James Young Simpson of Bathgate was the first to use chloroform in surgery and childbirth in 1847, while a member of the Faculty of Medicine at Edinburgh University. Later Lord Lister, of that same faculty, was a pioneer in the use of antiseptics to prevent infection. And Sir Alexander Fleming, born in Ayrshire, was the discoverer of penicillin in the 1920s.

Scots have gone all over the world to build roads, bridges, dams, and to make their fortunes in various ways. The one who made the greatest fortune was Andrew Carnegie of Dunfermline, who built an iron and steel empire in Pittsburgh, Pennsylvania in the nineteenth century. He became a major philanthropist—some said to atone for his ruthless ways in industry. Both in his adopted country and in his native land, the legacy of his vast fortune is particularly devoted to furthering education, which is so dear to the heart of every true Scot.

People of Scots descent are to be found all over the world. They exist in large numbers in the United States, New Zealand, and Canada—where McGill University in Montreal is named after James McGill who was born in 1744 and was educated at Glasgow University before emigrating to Canada to make his large fortune there. Immigrants from the west of Scotland helped found what is now known as Princeton University in the United States as an

The view Sir Walter Scott saw from Abbotsford, his home

institution to train Presbyterian ministers. One of its early presidents was John Witherspoon, who arrived there from Paisley in 1768. Witherspoon was the only clergyman to sign the Declaration of Independence.

The famous economist John Kenneth Galbraith has written a delightful book about growing up in Ontario, Canada, in a community where everyone, including his parents, was from Scotland. It is called *The Scotch* and has some very funny things to say about the character and customs of those transplanted Scots.

Somehow or other, wherever in the world they may find themselves, the Scots have a way of fitting into their surroundings without forgetting where their real heritage lies.

MAP KEY

Cities and Towns in Scotland

Aberchirder	C6	Cumnock	E4	Hurliness	B5	New Galloway	E4
Aberdeen	C6	Cupan	D6	Innerleithen	E5	Newton Stewart	F4
Aberfeldy	D5	Dair	E4	Insch	C6	Nigg	C5
Aberfoyle	D4	Dalbeattie	F5	Inveraray	D3	North Berwick	D6
Aboyne	C6	Daliburgh	C1	Inverbervie	D6	North Tolsta	B2
Acharacle	D3	Dalkeith	E5	Invergarry	C4	Oban	D3
Airdrie	E5	Dalmally	D4	Invergordon	C4	Old Meldrum	C6
Alford	C6	Dalmellington	E4	Inverness	C4	Oykel Bridge	C4
Alloa	D5	Dalry	E4	Inverurie	C6	Paisley	E4
Alness	C4	Dalwhinnie	D4	Irvine	E4	Peebles	E5
Altnaharra	B4	Dingwall	C4	Jedburgh	E6	Penicuik	E5
Alyth	D5	Dores	C4	John o'Groat's	B5	Perth	D5
Annan	F5	Dornie	C3	Keith	C6	Peterhead	C7
Applecross	C3	Dornoch	C4	Kelso	E6	Pierowall	A6
Arbroath	D6	Douglas	E5	Kilchoan	D2	Pitlochry	D5
Ardrossan	E4	Dounreay	B5	Killin	D4	Polbain	B3
Arisaig	D3	Drumbeg	B3	Kilmallie	D3	Poolewe	C3
Auchterarder	D5	Drummore	F4	Kilmarnock	E4	Portaskaig	E2
Aviemore	C5	Drymen	D4	Kilmelford	D3	Port Ellen	E2
Ayr	E4	Dufftown	C5	Kilsyth	E4	Port Glasgow	E4
Balallan	B2	Dumbarton	E4	Kinbrace	B5	Portmahomack	C5
Ballachulish	D3	Dumfries	E5	Kingussie	C4	Portnahaven	E2
Ballantrae	E4	Dunbar	E6	Kinlochewe	C3	Port of Ness	B2
Ballater	C5	Dunbeath	B5	Kinloch Hourn	C3	Portpatrick	F3
Ballinluig	D5	Dunblane	D5	Kinross	D5	Portree	C2
Balmoral Castle	C5	Dundee	D6	Kintore	C6	Portsoy	C6
Banchory	C6	Dunfermline	D5	Kirkcaldy	D5	Port William	F4
Banff	C6	Dunkeld	D5	Kirkcolm	F3	Prestwick	E4
Bankfoot	D5	Dunoon	E4	Kirkcudbright	F4	Rosehearty	C6
Barrhill	E4	Duns	E6	Kirkintilloch	E4	Rothes	C5
Barrhead	E4	Dunvegan	C2	Kirkton of Glenisla	D5	Rothesay	E3
Barvas	B2	Durness	B4	Kirkwall	B6	Rutherglen	E4
Bathgate	E5	Dyce	C6	Kirriemuir	D5	St. Andrews	D6
Bayble	B2	East Kilbride	E4	Kyle	C3	St. Margaret's Hope	B6
Beauly	C4	Echt	C6	Kylestrome	B3	Salen	D3
Bettyhill	B4	Edinburgh	E5	Ladybank	D5	Saltcoats	E4
Biggar	E5	Edzell	D6	Lagg	E3	Sanquhar	E5
Blair-Atholl	D5	Elgin	C5	Laide	C3	Scourie	B3
Blairgowrie	D5	Elgol	C2	Lairg	B4	Selkirk	E6
Bonar Bridge	C4	Ellon	C6	Lamlash	E3	Shieldaig	C3
Bowmore	E2	Evanton	C4	Lanark	E5	Sollas	C1
Bracadale	C2	Eyemouth	E6	Langholm	E6	South Queensferry	E5
Braemar	C5-D5	Fallkirk	E5	Largs	E4	Stewarton	E4
Brechin	D6	Fettercairn	D6	Lauder	E6	Stirling	D5
Brenish	B1	Findhorn	C5	Laurencekirk	D6	Stonehaven	D6
Broadford	C3	Fochabers	C5	Leith (part of Edinburgh)	E5	Strachur	D3
Brodick	E3	Ford	D3	Leven	D6	Strathaven	E4
Brora	B5	Forfar	D6	Linlithgow	E5	Stranraer	F3
Buckhaven	D5	Forres	C5	Lochaline	D3	Strichen	C6
Buckle	C6	Fort Augustus	C4	Lochcarron	C3	Strome Ferry	C3
Bunessan	D2	Fortrose	C4	Lochdonhead	D3	Stromness	B5
Burghead	C5	Fort William	D3	Lochearnhead	D4	Strontian	D3
Burntisland	D5	Fraserburgh	C7	Lochgilphead	D3	Tain	C4
Callander	D4	Gairloch	C3	Lochinver	B3	Tarbert	E3
Campbeltown	E3	Galashiels	E6	Lochmaben	E5	Tarbet	D4
Cannich	C4	Garmouth	C5	Lochranza	E3	Tarfside	D6
Carinish	C1	Garve	C4	Lockerbie	E5	Tarland	C6
Carloway	B2	Gatehouse-of-Fleet	F4	Lossiemouth	C5	Tarves	C6
Carluke	E5	Girvan	E4	Lumsden	C6	Tayport	D6
Carnostie	D6	Glasgow	E4	Lybster	B5	Teangue	C3
Carradak	E5	Glenbarr	E3	Macduff	C6	Thornhill	E5
Carr Bridge	C5	Glenelg	C3	Machrihanish	E3	Thurso	B5
Castlebay	D1	Glenfinnan	D3	Mallaig	D3	Tighnabruaich	E3
Castle Douglas	F5	Glenluce	F4	Mauchline	E4	Tillyfourie	C6
Cawdor	C5	Glenrothes	D5	Maud	C6	Tobermory	D2
Clydebank	E4	Golspie	C5	Maybole	E4	Tomintoul	C5
Coatbridge	E4-E5	Gowdenbeath	D5	Melvaig	C3	Tomgue	B4
Coldstream	E6	Grangemouth	D5	Millport	E4	Troon	E4
Coupar Angus	D5	Grantown-on-Spey	C5	Moffat	E5	Turriff	C6
Cove	C3	Greenlaw	E6	Moniaive	E5	Tyndrum	D4
Cowdenbeath	D5	Greenock	E4	Montrose	D6	Uig	B2
Craighouse	E3	Gretna	F5	Motherwell	E5	Uig	C2
Crail	D6	Haddington	E6	Moy	C4	Ullapool	C3
Crieff	D5	Hamilton	E4	Muirkirk	E4	Whitehouse	C6
Crinan	D3	Harris	D2	Musselburgh	E5	Whithorn	F4
Cromarty	C4	Hawick	E6	Nairn	C5	Whiting Bay	E3
Crossbost	B2	Helensburgh	D4	Nethy Bridge	C5	Wick	B5
Cruden Bay	C7	Helmsdale	B5	Newburgh	C7	Wigtown	F4
Cullen	C6	Huntly	C6	New Cumnock	E4	Wishaw	E5

MINI-FACTS AT A GLANCE

GENERAL INFORMATION

Official Language: English

Other Languages: Gaelic is mostly spoken in the Highlands and the Western Isles; Scots, a dialect more widely used, contains many words that do not exist in English.

Government: Scotland is part of the United Kingdom, which is a constitutional monarchy. The monarch (currently Queen Elizabeth II) is head of the government in name only. The prime minister, an elected official, is the actual head. He or she is the leader of the majority political party and heads a cabinet of ministers (what in the United States is called a cabinet of secretaries) of various departments.

The legislature, called Parliament, is made up of the monarch, the House of Lords and the House of Commons. The members of the Commons (known as M.P.s — members of Parliament) are elected; this house is the governing body of the legislature. The maximum term for a session of Parliament is five years, but the prime minister can call an election at any time and often does, before the term is up. The Lords are bishops of the Church of England; hereditary and created peers (lords, earls, dukes); and law Lords. This body has little real power but can voice its views on current affairs. Many of the created peers are former members of the Commons whose services to party politics are rewarded by lifetime peerages, which means the titles do not descend to their children. The House of Lords may be appealed to as a Supreme Court in the judicial system.

Scotland sends 71 elected members to the House of Commons, a 635-member body. All Scottish peers do not attend the Lords, but elect 16 of their number to represent them.

Scotland has its own chief executive, called the Secretary of State for Scotland, who is appointed by the prime minister. The secretary's office is called the Scottish Office and has five main departments — Agriculture and Fisheries, Economic Planning, Development (housing, public utilities, and transportation), Education, and Home and Health (criminal justice, police and fire protection, prisons, and public health).

Scotland's local government, judicial, and educational systems are different from those in England, Wales, and Northern Ireland. The country is divided into seven regions and the island groups of Orkney, Shetland, and the Western Isles.

The Scottish judicial system is based on Roman law, unlike America's and England's, which are based on common law. Roman law is based on established, written laws, whereas common law is based on precedents that are the result of earlier court cases.

Flag: The national flag, called St. Andrew's Cross, is blue with a white, saltire (X-shaped) cross on it. Although it has not been officially adopted, it is used all over Scotland. It forms part of the Union Jack, the United Kingdom's flag.

National Song: "God Save the Queen," the national anthem of all of Great Britain

Religion: The Church of Scotland, the kirk, is also known as the Presbyterian church. But while Scotland has a national church, religious freedom is guaranteed. There are Protestants of other denominations, Roman Catholics, Jews, and many Indians and Pakistanis who have settled in Scotland practice their own religions.

Money: The basic unit of currency in Scotland is the pound, which is equal to 100 new pence. As of March 1985, one pound equaled $1.08 in United States currency. Scotland has its own banks whose bank notes are treated as foreign currency in England. The English one-pound note is being abolished and replaced by a coin. Scotland retains its one-pound notes.

Weights and Measures: Scotland uses the imperial system of weights and measures, the same system traditionally used in the United States. Conversion to the metric system is in progress.

Population: 5,117,146 (1981 census)

Cities: The largest cities in Scotland are:

Glasgow	733,794
Edinburgh	439,672
Aberdeen	215,246
Dundee	177,674

(Population figures based on 1985 census.)

GEOGRAPHY

Highest Point: Ben Nevis, 4,406 ft. (1,343 m)

Lowest Point: Sea level along the coast

Rivers: The longest river is the Tay, 120 mi. (193 km) long. The most important river is the Clyde.

Lakes: Loch Lomond, 23 mi. (37 km) long and 5 mi. (8 km) wide at its widest point, is the largest lake.

Mountains: Two main mountain ranges lie in the northern part of Scotland called the Highlands. They are the Grampian Mountains and the Northwest Highlands.

Greatest Distances: North to south, 274 mi. (441 km)
East to west, 154 mi. (248 km)

Area: 30,416 sq. mi. (78,777 km²)

NATURE

Vegetation: Many of the original forests in Scotland have been cleared for cultivation, but there is an active Forestry Commission that plants new trees. Except in the northernmost parts, there are many lushly wooded areas—often called glens. The abundance of shrubs and flowers found in Scotland include rhododendrons, fuchsias, and the famous Scottish heather. A prickly shrub with brilliant yellow blossoms, called whin in Scotland (gorse in England), is also widespread. In the springtime daffodils, snowdrops, and yellow primroses grow wild in the woods. The most common wild berry is the bramble (blackberry). In the Highlands and islands, peat is plentiful. This is a composite of soil and decayed vegetation such as reeds and moss. It has been used for centuries as domestic fuel and still is in the Outer Hebrides. Its main use nowadays is in the distilling of whiskey and the smoking of fish. In woods, along loch sides, and in many countryside areas there grow the large, strong ferns known as bracken. These, unfortunately, harbor many flies, including tiny ones called midges whose bite some people call "the curse of Scotland."

Fish: There is an abundance of seafood along the coast of Scotland, including herring, haddock, cod, sole, crab, and lobster. In the rivers can be found salmon, trout, and salmon trout.

Animals: There are as many as 500,000 red deer in Scotland. Other wild animals include otters, pine martens, wildcats, foxes, badgers, rabbits, hares, and seals, off the coast.

Birds: The many varieties of birds include golden eagles, falcons, buzzards, kestrels, and ospreys. There are also seabirds such as gannets, fulmars, puffins, and sea gulls.

EVERYDAY LIFE

Food: The most famous Scottish foods are haggis—which is traditionally eaten on Burns Night—Scotch broth, and shortbread.

Some Scots eat their main meal in the middle of the day and have high tea at 5:30 or 6:00 in the evening. This means something cooked, like bacon and eggs, sausages, or fish and chips, besides a selection of breads and what the Scots call teabread—sweet rolls, scones, crumpets—and perhaps a cake or little fancy cakes.

Some households have afternoon tea at 4:00 and dinner or supper at 7:00 or 7:30 in the evening. Afternoon tea is like high tea minus the cooked course. The Scots drink a lot of tea at all times of the day.

Large amounts of mutton are eaten in Scotland and there is fine beef from the Aberdeen Angus cattle. Fish is also a favorite because there is a great variety and it is plentiful. Herring is very popular and inexpensive. Scottish salmon is much loved, but expensive.

Housing: Much of the housing in Scotland is old and ranges from little stone cottages in the Highlands to elegant houses and apartments in the cities. There is also much housing built between the two world wars and since World War II. This includes many houses built by local authorities and rented out. Many slum areas, such as those in the city of Glasgow, were cleared in recent years and replaced by whole new towns. Although the slums were terrible, many of the people relocated in the clean new towns feel they are not as friendly and complain about the lack of community. Most of the substantial old apartments (called flats) in the cities are owned by their occupants. Many of the large old houses have been converted into apartments. In certain areas, however, housing shortages are a problem.

Holidays:

>January 1-2, New Year
>Good Friday
>Easter Monday
>First Monday in May, Labour Day
>Last Monday in May, Spring Holiday
>First Monday in August, August Bank Holiday
>December 25, Christmas

Culture: There is a rich heritage of poetry in Scotland. The earliest poets were unknown bards. The earliest Scottish written literature was in the old Scots dialect, the equivalent of Chaucer's English.

Robert Burns, who lived in the eighteenth century, is the national poet of Scotland. He wrote mainly in the Scottish dialect. One of his best known poems is "To a Mouse." It has the famous lines: "The best laid schemes o' mice and men / Gang aft a-gley (go often awry)."

Sir Walter Scott, also an eighteenth-century writer, is the second most famous literary figure in Scotland. He, like Burns, sought to preserve the Scottish language and traditions. He is famous for the Waverley novels, of which the best known is *Ivanhoe*.

Robert Louis Stevenson, who was born in Scotland, but who spent many years in America and Samoa, is most famous for *Treasure Island*, *Kidnapped*, and *The Strange Case of Dr. Jekyll and Mr. Hyde*.

Twentieth-century writers include poet Hugh McDiarmid, who led a movement to revive writing in Lallans (a Lowland Scots dialect); Lewis Grassic Gibbon, who wrote a trilogy of Scottish life called *A Scots Quair* (one of the three novels became a television play called "Sunset Song"); and John Buchan, who wrote *The Thirty-nine Steps* and *Greenmantle*.

Scotland has contributed much to films also. Actors David Niven and Deborah Kerr both were born in Scotland, as was Sean Connery, the first James Bond. Director Bill Forsyth, who makes films in Scotland about Scotland, has gained fame with *Gregory's Girl*, *Local Hero*, and *Comfort and Joy*.

Scotland has had many important painters, including Allan Ramsay and Sir Henry Raeburn, who lived in the eighteenth and nineteenth centuries.

Musically, the most unique contribution Scotland has made to the world has been bagpipe music, which varies from marches to dance music. Sad songs or warlike tunes are called *pibrochs*; they are classified as "big music." "Little music" includes the accompaniments to Scottish dances, such as the reel and the Highland fling.

Sports and Recreation: The Scots are very fond of dancing, both modern and traditional. Of the latter, the eightsome reel is most popular. Two other old favorites are the Highland fling and the sword dance, which is danced over two crossed swords. These dances are most often done to bagpipe music.

Golf, which originated in Scotland in the twelfth century, is its most widely played game. Many courses are very scenic as they often run along the coastline.

The favorite spectator sport is soccer—or football, as it is called in Britain. There are many amateur teams and soccer is played at most schools. Some rugby football, or rugger, is played but it has not captured people's interest the way soccer has.

Lawn bowls, a game in which large, carefully balanced bowling balls are rolled across a green toward a small, white target ball called the jack, also has many players. A similar game called curling is played on ice.

The Scots also love to hike, ski, sail, bicycle, fish, and hunt. There is good fishing in the lochs, streams, and along the coast. Hunting of deer, grouse, and pheasant is activity for the well-to-do.

Communication: In Scotland there are two TV networks—the BBC (British Broadcasting Corporation) and Scottish Television Limited, which is overseen by the Independent Broadcasting Authority (formerly Independent Television Authority). Owners of TV sets must pay license fees every year. This money goes to support the BBC, which is public television with no commercials. Even though Scottish TV Limited does run commercials, advertisers do not sponsor programs.

The four national radio networks run by the BBC include Radio Scotland. In addition, there are independent local radio stations such as Radio Clyde, broadcasting from Glasgow.

Some people in Scotland read newspapers that circulate throughout Britain, such as the *London Times* or the *Daily Mirror*. Most read one or more of the nine Scottish dailies, of which the most important are *The Scotsman* (Edinburgh) and the *Glasgow Herald*. Although there is freedom of the press in Britain, journalists must be careful not to break the libel laws. These are even stricter in Scotland than in England.

Pronunciation: The Scots, like most people, prefer visitors to pronounce the names of places and cities correctly. Here are some examples:

Aberdeen   (ah • bur • DEAN)
Argyll   (r • GILE)
Braemar   (bray • MAHR)
Caithness   (cayth • NESS)
Cuillin Hills   (COO • lin)
Culzean Castle   (cul • AIN)
Dundee   (dun • DEE)
Edinburgh   (ED • in • bur • ra)
Eigg   (EGG)
Glasgow   (GLAZ • goh)
Inverness   (in • ver • NESS)
Kintyre   (kin • TIRE)
Kirriemuir   (kir • ree • MEWER)

Transportation: In recent years, many new roads, including expressways, have been built in Britain. In 1980, there were 30,726 mi. (49,499 km) of roads in Scotland.

There is also an excellent railroad system, including the Glasgow subway. Train travel between cities is among the best in the world. Recently the British Railways Board inaugurated the world's fastest diesel rail service—Inter-City-125 between London and Edinburgh. British railroads are, for the most part, nationalized, although there are still a few small privately owned passenger railroads.

Recently, there has been a revival of interest in the use of inland waterways for recreation and freight. Major Scottish ports are on the rivers Forth and Clyde, plus the new oil ports in Orkney and Shetland.

There are major airports in Aberdeen, Edinburgh, and Glasgow.

Education: The Scottish Educational Department and local authorities are in charge of education.

Education in Scotland always has been more democratic than in England. Scotland does not have the equivalent of the public schools (which are really private) like England's Eton or Harrow. Of the private schools in Scotland, very few are boarding schools.

Schooling is compulsory for children between the ages of five and sixteen. There are different options for courses of study. Some schools, for example, take students at eleven and graduate them at eighteen. Senior comprehensive schools take students aged twelve, thirteen, or fourteen; the course of study lasts until they are eighteen. A comprehensive school is one that offers courses in academic as well as vocational subjects. The growth in the number of comprehensive schools in recent years represents a change in Scotland's school system. In the past, many more students went to either an academic or a vocational school. At present, most secondary schools are six-year comprehensives.

Students may leave secondary school after four years. If they pass a test after five or six years of secondary school, they are eligible for a university or for professional training not taught in a university setting, such as courses in architecture, engineering, or social work.

There are eight universities in Scotland: Aberdeen, Stirling, Dundee, Edinburgh, Glasgow, Heriot-Watt (Edinburgh), Strathclyde, and St. Andrews.

Another option for higher education is the "Open University." It offers courses on a part-time basis via radio, TV, correspondence courses, and summer school.

Health: The National Health Service is a system of socialized medicine. This means that everyone who is a resident of Britain can receive free medical care.

Health has been improving in Britain in recent years. Tuberculosis is practically nonexistent; the infant mortality rate is low. However, as in other parts of the world, cancer and heart disease are major health problems.

Principal Products:
Agriculture: Oats, barley, wheat, sheep, cattle,
Manufacturing: Automobiles, chemicals, industrial machinery, iron and steel, ships, textiles, whiskey

IMPORTANT DATES

First century A.D.—First recorded mention of Scotland in writings of Tacitus

A.D. 80—Roman army invades Scotland and conquers Picts

83—Battle of Mons Graupius

84—Agricola withdraws from Caledonia

120s—Hadrian's Wall built

208—Emperor Severus comes as far north as the Moray Firth, meets constant guerrilla resistance

563—Saint Columba founds a Christian mission on the island of Iona

800s—Vikings first invade north of Scotland

843—Kenneth MacAlpin declares himself king of all territory north of the Forth (his kingdom becomes known as Scotia)

1040—Duncan killed by Macbeth

1093—Malcolm III killed by the Normans who conquered England in 1066

1124—David I becomes king and brings a measure of stability to Scotland

1170s—William the Lion forms alliance with France, fails in attempt to invade England; Scotland comes under feudal subjection to England

1189—William the Lion buys back Scotland's independence from England

1263—Battle of Largs; Norwegians give up claim to Hebrides

1286—Alexander III's three-year-old granddaughter Margaret becomes queen

1292—Edward I wins Battle of Dunbar

1297—William Wallace defeats large part of English army at Battle of Stirling Bridge

1305—Wallace captured by Edward I and executed

1306—Robert the Bruce crowned king of Scotland

1314—Robert the Bruce defeats the English at Battle of Bannockburn

1320—Scotland declares independence from England

1328—The English recognize Scottish independence

1371—Robert Stewart becomes the first Stewart king (spelling later changed to Stuart)

1424—James I returns to Scotland after being held hostage by the English for eighteen years

1437—James I stabbed to death

1455—James II attempts to restore order to Scotland

1460—James II killed at siege of Roxburgh

1488—James III thrown from his horse and stabbed to death

1503—James IV marries Margaret Tudor, an English princess

1507—First printing press established in Edinburgh

1513—James IV killed at Battle of Flodden Field

1542—Scotland invaded by English army sent by Henry VIII; James V dies trying to counter-invade; his daughter Mary is born

1557—The First Covenant, renouncing the Catholic church, drawn up by a group of Scottish nobles

1558—Mary, Queen of Scots, who was sent to France at age six, marries the Dauphin, son of the king of France

1561—Mary, widowed, returns to assume throne of Scotland

1567—Mary forced to abdicate in favor of her one-year-old son

1587—Mary executed by Queen Elizabeth I of England, her cousin

1603—James VI, son of Mary, also becomes James I of England after death of Elizabeth I

1625—Charles I becomes king

1638—Group of Scots sign the National Covenant

1642—Beginning of English civil war; Scottish Covenanters support Cromwell against Charles I

1649—Charles I beheaded

1650—Charles I's son, Charles II, crowned king in Scotland

1651—Charles II, defeated by Cromwell at the Battle of Dunbar, flees abroad

1654—Cromwell forces Scots to unite with England

1660—Charles II restored to throne of England and Scotland

1688—James VII, deposed, flees to France

1707—The Act of Union joins Scotland with England and Wales, forming the United Kingdom of Great Britain

1715—First Jacobite rebellion, in support of the son of exiled James VII, put down by the English

1744—Prince Charles Edward, grandson of James VII, returns to Scotland; Jacobites rally to his cause

1746—Prince Charles Edward defeated by the English at the Battle of Culloden Moor; he escapes to live abroad

1746 onward—Highland Clearances; breakup of clans; thousands forced to emigrate or move to cities

1822—George IV visits Scotland, establishes lasting relationship between monarchy and Scotland

1852—Prince Albert, consort of Queen Victoria, buys and restores Balmoral Castle, now the royal summer residence

1934—Scottish National party formed

1970—A British petroleum company strikes oil under the sea east of Aberdeen. This begins the most significant industrial development in Scotland in this century

1975—Counties in Scotland are reorganized into regional units of local government

1979—The Scottish National party, or "home rule party," loses 9 of its 11 seats in Parliament.

1980—Small towns in eastern Scotland report almost full employment because of oil-related industrialization.

1983—The Scottish National party, which advocates home rule as a step towards independence for Scotland, retains its two seats in Parliament.

IMPORTANT PEOPLE

James Adam (1730-94), interior designer

Robert Adam (1728-92), architect of Charlotte Square in Edinburgh

Gnaeus Julius Agricola (A.D. 40-93), Roman governor of Britain

Alexander III (1241-86), king of Scotland whose daughter married Eric, king of Norway, thus making peace between the two countries

John Balliol (1249-1315), contender for Scottish throne, accepted overlordship of Edward I of England

John Barbour (1325?-95), poet, wrote the *Brus,* an epic about Robert Bruce

J.M. Barrie (1860-1937), novelist and playwright, author of *Peter Pan*

Alexander Graham Bell (1847-1922), Scottish-born American inventor of the telephone

James Boswell (1740-95), biographer of Samuel Johnson

Earl of Bothwell (James Hepburn) (1536?-78), third husband of Mary, Queen of Scots

Robert Bruce (1210-95), competitor with John Balliol for Scottish throne

Robert the Bruce (Robert I) (1274-1329), king of Scotland, defeated the English at Bannockburn in 1314

John Buchan (Lord Tweedsmuir) (1875-1940), author, governor-general of Canada from 1935-40

Robert Burns (1759-96), most famous Scottish poet

Thomas Carlyle (1795-1881), historian

Andrew Carnegie (1835-1919), Scottish-born American industrialist

Charles I (1600-49), Stuart king who was beheaded

Charles II (1630-85), king of Britain following the restoration of the Stuarts

Prince Charles Edward (1720-88), known as Bonnie Prince Charlie

Saint Columba (521-97), missionary who founded Christian mission on island of Iona in 563

Sean Connery (1930-   ), movie actor, the first to play James Bond

Oliver Cromwell (1599-1658), leader of the revolution against the Stuarts

Duke of Cumberland (William Augustus) (1721-65), son of George II, military leader who put down Jacobite uprising

David Daiches (1912-   ), author, critic, biographer

Lord Darnley (1545-67), second husband of Mary, Queen of Scots

David I (Earl of Northampton and Huntingdon) (1084-1153), king of Scotland who brought stability back to Scotland after a period of unrest

David II (1324-71), king of Scotland, son of Robert the Bruce

William Dunbar (1460?-1520), poet

Duncan I (d. 1040), conquered much of mainland Scotland

John Duns Scotus (1265?-1308), theologian whose name came to mean a stupid person (dunce)

Edward I (1239-1307), king of England, fought against Scotland

Edward II (1284-1327), king of England, defeated by Robert the Bruce

Elizabeth I (1533-1603), queen of England who had Mary, Queen of Scots, executed

Sir Alexander Fleming (1881-1955), scientist, discoverer of penicillin

Bill Forsyth (   ), movie director whose credits include *Gregory's Girl*

John Kenneth Galbraith (1908-   ), Canadian-born economist of Scottish ancestry

John Grierson (1898-1972), documentary filmmaker of the 1940s

Sir James Guthrie (1859-1930), portrait painter

Hadrian (76-138), Roman emperor who built a wall to try to contain the Caledonians

Henry II (1133-89), king of England, forced King David I to return Northumbria to England

Henry VIII (1491-1547), English king who sent troops to Scotland

Robert Henryson (1430?-1506?), poet

David Hume (1711-76), philosopher, wrote *A Treatise on Human Nature*

Gordon Jackson (1924-   ), actor

James I (1394-1437), Scottish king who helped Joan of Arc against the English

James II (1430-60), Scottish king

James III (1451-88), Scottish king

James IV (1473-1513), Scottish king slain at Flodden Field

James V (1512-42), Scottish king, father of Mary, Queen of Scots

James VI (1566-1625), Scottish king who also became James I of England, sponsor of the King James version of the Bible

James VII (James II of England) (1633-1701), Scottish king who, because he was Catholic, was replaced by William of Orange

James Edward (1688-1766), son of James VII, known as the "Old Pretender" to the throne, one of the last of the Stuarts

Joan (1321-62), queen of Scotland, sister of English king Edward III

Deborah Kerr (1921-   ), Scottish-born movie actress

John Knox (1505-72), founder of Protestantism in Scotland

Sir Harry Lauder (1870-1950), entertainer

Lord Lister (1827-1912), scientist who made discoveries in antiseptics

David Livingstone (1831-73), explorer of central Africa

Kenneth MacAlpin (d. 858?), king of the Scots of Dalriada

Macbeth (d. 1057), Scottish king immortalized in the Shakespeare play

Flora Macdonald (1722-90), woman who helped Bonnie Prince Charlie escape the English

James Ramsay MacDonald (1866-1937), first Labour party British prime minister

Charles Macintosh (1766-1843), inventor of the raincoat

Sir Compton Mackenzie (1883-1972), novelist, author of *Tight Little Island* (title in Scotland: *Whisky Galore*)

Charles Rennie Mackintosh (1868-1928), architect and designer

Kirkpatrick Macmillan (1810-1878), inventor of the bicycle

Malcolm III (d. 1093), killed Macbeth, was Duncan I's son

Malcolm IV (1141-65), Scottish king, son of David I

Margaret (1046-93), wife of Malcolm III

Margaret (1283-90), daughter of the king of Norway, Eric II, and queen of Scotland

Mary, Queen of Scots (1542-87), executed by Elizabeth I, her cousin

John McAdam (1756-1836), inventor of tar surface for roads

Ewan McColl (   ), folk singer

Hugh McDiarmid (Christopher Murray Grieve, real name) (1892-1978), modern poet

James McGill (1744-1813), Scottish-born Canadian for whom McGill University in Canada is named, businessman and philanthropist

James Leslie Mitchell (Lewis Grassic Gibbon) (1901-35), author, wrote *A Scots Quair*

Saint Ninian (360?-432), early Christian missionary in Scotland

David Niven (1910-83), Scottish-born movie actor

John Pettie (1839-93), painter

Sir Henry Raeburn (1756-1823), portrait painter

Allan Ramsay (1713-84), portrait painter

Jean Redpath (   ), modern folk singer

Jeanie Ritchie (1922-   ), modern folk singer

David Rizzio (1533?-66), Mary, Queen of Scots' secretary, murdered by her husband, Lord Darnley

Robert II (1316-90), first Stewart (later Stuart) king, crowned 1371

Robert Stewart (1340?-1420), Robert II's son, regent of Scotland

Sir Walter Scott (1771-1832), poet and historical novelist

Sir James Young Simpson (1811-70), discovered the use of chloroform for surgery and childbirth

Adam Smith (1723-90), philosopher/economist, author of *The Wealth of Nations*

Robert Louis Stevenson (1850-94), novelist, author of *Treasure Island* and *The Strange Case of Dr. Jekyll and Mr. Hyde*

Tacitus (55?-after 117), Roman historian who first wrote about Scotland

Robert William Thomson (1822-73), engineer, inventor of the pneumatic tire

Margaret Tudor (1489-1541), wife of James IV, queen of Scotland, daughter of Henry VII of England

William Wallace (1272?-1305), patriot, defeated English army but executed by the English

James Watt (1736-1819), developer of the steam engine

Sir David Wilkie (1785-1841), painter

William the Lion (1143-1214), Scottish king who formed an alliance with France and tried to invade England

William of Orange (1650-1702), king of England after James VII was deposed

John Witherspoon (1723-94), early president of Princeton University in America

RULERS OF SCOTLAND

Kenneth MacAlpin	843-60	Alexander I	1107-24
Donald I	860-63	David I	1124-53
Constantine I	863-77	Malcolm IV	1153-65
Aedh	877-78	William the Lion	1165-1214
Eocha	878-89	Alexander II	1214-49
Donald II	889-900	Alexander III	1249-86
Constantine II	900-43	Margaret, the Maid	
Malcolm I	943-54	of Norway	1286-90
Indulphus	954-62	First Interregnum	1290-92
Duff	962-67	John Balliol	1292-96
Colin	967-71	Second Interregnum	1296-1306
Kenneth II	971-95	Robert the Bruce	1306-29
Constantine III	995-97	David II	1329-71
Kenneth III	997-1005	Robert II	1371-90
Malcolm II	1005-34	Robert III	1390-1406
Duncan I	1034-40	James I	1406-37
Macbeth	1040-57	James II	1437-60
Malcolm III	1057-93	James III	1460-88
Donald Bane	1093-94	James IV	1488-1513
Duncan II	1094	James V	1513-42
Donald Bane (again)	1094-97	Mary, Queen of Scots	1542-67
Edgar	1097-1107	James VI	1567-1603

A Scottish farm

RULERS OF SCOTLAND AND ENGLAND

James VI, I of England	1603-25
Charles I	1625-49
Commonwealth	1649-60
Charles II	1660-85
James VII, II of England	1685-88
William III	1688-1702
and Mary II	1688-94
Anne	1702-14
George I	1714-27
George II	1727-60
George III	1760-1820
George IV	1820-30
William IV	1830-37
Victoria	1837-1901
Edward VII	1901-10
George V	1910-36
Edward VIII	1936 (abdicated before coronation)
George VI	1936-52
Elizabeth II	1952-

INDEX

Page numbers that appear in boldface type indicate illustrations

About the Author

Dorothy B. Sutherland comes from Glasgow, Scotland (which makes her a Glaswegian) and was educated there at Hillhead High School and Glasgow University. She has lived in Hamburg, Germany; London, England; and in New York and Chicago. She was advertising and publicity manager for the University of Chicago Press for several years and has had her own company, working with various publishers, since 1969. She has written both book reviews and articles about publishing for *Publishers Weekly* and *Saturday Review* and has taken part in seminars and conducted a class on publishing.

She has two red-headed daughters (red hair is a true Scottish characteristic). She has frequently given parties on Robert Burns birthday at which she practices her inborn skill at making Scotch broth.